OUR BEAUTIFUL MIND

PRINCE MICHAEL OWOKOYA

OUR BEAUTIFUL MIND

Copyright © 2022 Prince Michael Owokoya.

All rights reserved. No part of this book may be used or reproduced by any means, graphic, electronic, or mechanical, including photocopying, recording, taping or by any information storage retrieval system without the written permission of the author except in the case of brief quotations embodied in critical articles and reviews.

iUniverse books may be ordered through booksellers or by contacting:

iUniverse
1663 Liberty Drive
Bloomington, IN 47403
www.iuniverse.com
844-349-9409

Because of the dynamic nature of the Internet, any web addresses or links contained in this book may have changed since publication and may no longer be valid. The views expressed in this work are solely those of the author and do not necessarily reflect the views of the publisher, and the publisher hereby disclaims any responsibility for them.

Any people depicted in stock imagery provided by Getty Images are models, and such images are being used for illustrative purposes only.
Certain stock imagery © Getty Images.

ISBN: 978-1-6632-3579-4 (sc)
ISBN: 978-1-6632-4335-5 (hc)
ISBN: 978-1-6632-4334-8 (e)

Library of Congress Control Number: 2022914261

Print information available on the last page.

iUniverse rev. date: 08/31/2022

This book is dedicated to the memory of my late mother, Princess Adeite Tejuola Owokoya. My Goddess. The love of my life. Without you I am not me.

Our Beautiful Mind

God is great,

God is beautiful,

God is awesome—

Excellence in his creations.

He who creates us in his image,

He who creates our beautiful mind,

Our beautiful mind—

The mind of God.

The mind that cogitates and strategizes,

The mind that conceives and actualizes,

The mind that dreams and implements,

The mind that perceives and predicts,

The mind that develops and achieves,

The mind that empathizes and sympathizes.

God is great,

God is beautiful,

God is awesome—

Excellence in his creations.

He who creates us in his image,

He who creates our beautiful mind,

Our beautiful mind—

The mind of God.

The mind that forgives and compliments,

The mind that plans and accomplishes,

The mind that promotes and advances,

The mind that triumphs and celebrates,

The mind that knows right from wrong.

Our beautiful mind is the mind of God.

Uniqueness is a blessing. Blessing is a distinction. Distinction is ascendancy. It's not just what you have; it's who you are. It's not just how you are; it's what you are. It's not just the symbols you are created with. it's also the dynamism you possess. It's inscribed in your ethos. It's embedded in your personality. It's displayed in your representations. It's expressed in your pronouncements. It's apparent in your dispositions. It's obvious in your disciplines. It's established in your attitudes. It's ascertained in your mannerisms.

It's in your aura. It's in your bloodline. It's in your preeminence. When you are distinct, you are blessed with unparalleled qualities that are irreplaceable. With indisputable upsides that are irreproachable.

Everyone in our circles bring something more distinctive to the table. Everyone in our circles bring something more peculiar to the table. Everyone in our circles bring something more resourceful to the table. Everyone in our circles bring something more exciting, bring something more challenging to the table. Different from our own repertoire. Different from our own experiences. Different from our own preoccupations.

We can't be afraid of our own. We can't run away from ourselves. We definitely can't run away from our own people.

Would You Hold My Hand?

Would you hold my hand

And be my friend?

Would you hold my hand

And be my friend?

Would you please hold my hand

And be my friend today?

A friend in needs,

And a friend in deeds.

A friend to walk with,

And a friend to dine with.

A friend to talk to,

And a friend to confide in.

A good friend

Who has my back

In the open.

A great friend

Who has my front

In the dark corridors.

A friend who cares.

A good friend

Who covers my blind spots.

Are you a good friend,

A friend who leads,

A friend who sacrifices?

A friend who forgives,

A friend who compliments,

A friend who is considerate,

A friend who is passionate?

A friend to go to battle with,

A friend to go to war for,

A friend who loves others

Just as much as he loves himself?

A humble and selfless friend?

Would you hold my hand?

Would you hold my hand?

Would you please hold my hand

And be my friend today?

You can't stand alone. You shouldn't stand alone. You can't stand alone. Nobody should stand alone. You can't stand alone. It's foolishness to be all alone. What is the point of being all alone? What is the significance of being all alone? Poor, hungry, cynical, ignorant, pessimistic, close-minded, miserable. Nobody should stand alone, all by himself.

What you are not, you are not. What you are not, you don't replicate.

Who you are not, you are not. Who you are not, you don't represent. What you are not, you don't replicate.

Who you are not, you don't represent. What you are not, you don't duplicate. Represent what you truly are. Replicate who you truly are. You are who you are, you are, what you are. Stop being duplicitous. Just represent your true self through displays of your excellence, through displays of your best abilities.

Your life is absolutely the way you make it. Your life is absolutely about your personal efforts.

Your life is absolutely about your personal performances. When you make it, good. You will also enjoy all the rewards that come along with it. When you make it, great. You will also enjoy all the satisfaction that comes along with the extra commitments to be better than yesterday.

It's always about taking those extra steps that will convey you to the pinnacle of the mountaintops. Into the parlors of distinctiveness. Into the bedrooms of unparalleled comforts.

When It's Right

When it's right, It's right.

When it's wrong, It's wrong.

When it's right,

It's absolutely right.

When it's wrong,

It's definitely wrong.

The same accolades.

The same retributions.

The same celebrations.

The same condemnations.

The same rewards.

The same penalties.

When it's wrong,

It's wrong.

When it's right,

It's right.

When it's wrong,
It's always wrong.

When it's right, it's
absolutely right.

The same measurements.

The same calibrations.

The same judgments.

The same rewards.

The same penalties.

The same accolades.

When it's right,

It always right.

When it's wrong.

It's absolutely
wrong.

When it's right,
It's always right.

Life is a grind. Life is a struggle. Life is a celebration. Life is fun. Life is only for the living. To be here, among the living, irrespective of our situations. Still worthy of the struggles. To be here among the living, irrespective of our conditions. Still worthy of the challenges. To be here among the living, Irrespective of our statures. Still worthy of the celebrations.

We can only walk as far as we can go. We can only go as far as we can see. We can only see as far as we can go. We can only succeed as far as our knowledge. We can only be comfortable as far as our efforts. We can only be self-contented as far as our performances. We can only be special as far as our integrity.

Light is a powerful force over darkness when it refuses to shine. Darkness forever remains the same. When it refuses to sparkle, when it refuses to illuminate. Darkness forever remains the same. Rigid, impenetrable. Unapproachable, difficult. Just like ignorance over knowledge. Just like sentiment over realism. Just like superstition over factuality.

You know what to do. Just do it. Do whatever you have to do to empower your mind away from the shackles of depression. Do whatever you have to do to emancipate yourself from the shackles of ignorance. Do whatever you have to do to release your mind from the shackles of failures.

Do whatever you have to do to elevate your mind from the shackles of poverty. Do whatever you have to do to disentangle your mind from the shackles of despondency.

Everything in Life Matters

Everything in life matters.

Everything in life is important.

Everything in life matters.

Everything in life is significant.

Everything in life is important; everything in life is essential.

There is no coincidence.

There is no retrogression.

There is no turning back.

There is no ambiguity.

There is no failure.

There is no sorrow; there is no regret.

Every decision is critical.

Every action is relevant.

Every reaction is contentious.

Every mistake is pernicious; every progress is empowerment; every triumph is a celebration.

Every victory is a blessing.

It's absolutely within the laws, within the norms, within the traits of humanity. To be genuinely nice, to be loving, to be hospitable, to be truthful are absolutely within the core values. Within the cultures, within the traditions of humanity. To be candid, to be engaging, to be hardworking, to be resourceful, to be caring to himself, to everybody around him. It says everything about him. It says everything about his upbringing. It says everything about his character. It says everything about his beliefs. It says everything about his exposures. It says everything about his integrity, about his attributes. It says everything about his beautiful mindset.

Use your mind brilliantly to find solutions to your challenges. Use your spirit intelligently to empower your thinking in to preeminence. Control your emotions calmly to complement your distinctions in to exceptionalism. We are all endowed with excellent minds, with brilliant mindsets. Our minds are the catalysts to the greatness of our destinies.

A negative mind is counterproductive to a beautiful destiny. A brilliant mind is a game changer for a mediocre expectation. A mind positively utilized produces ascendancy. A mind positively utilized produces ingenuity. A mind positively utilized produces exceptionalism.

People around us are the most important people in our lives at any given time. When we invest positively in their lives, the dividend will be enormous. When we love them affectionately, the rewards will be overwhelming. When we respect their opinions, their trust will be immeasurable. When we lead them righteously; their loyalties will be unprecedented. When we compliment them honestly and candidly, our positive impacts on them will last forever.

If we do one thing right, we can always do everything right. It's about our mindsets, believing in ourselves to always do everything right.

It's not as far as we've come that's significant in how much further we still have to go.

Show Me How to Grow

Show me how to grow;

I promise I will be fruitful.

Teach me your ways;

I promise I will be self-accomplished.

Impact me with disciplines;

I promise I will exhibit distinctions.

Show me love;

I promise I will display compassion.

Teach me manners;

I promise I will uphold your principles.

Show me leadership;

I promise I will be an excellent follower.

Your greatness is in your distinctions. Your beauty is in your uniqueness. You can be good in a lot of things, but you still have to be great in the one thing you do best.

Repetition makes perfection. To be an exception, you have to continuously work on yourself so that you can be better than yesterday. So that you can be more victorious than ever before.

It's all in your mind, just the way you see it. If you see your life as beautiful, it's because your life is beautiful in your sight. If you see your life as beautiful, it's because your life is magnificent in your mindset.

Self-contentment: I don't care about what you have. I am very proud of mine. Even if not as much, I am still very proud of what I've got.

You don't really know yourself until you find yourself. You don't really know yourself until you find your uniqueness. Not until you find your progress, not until you find your goals, not until you find your strengths, not until you find your passions, not until you find your happiness, not until you find your destinations, not until you find your destiny.

Today matters. Today matters the most. More important than yesterday. More significant than tomorrow. Take care of today. Tomorrow will take care of itself.

When you do what you're supposed to do. When you're supposed to do it, you will always get the results you're supposed to get. When you don't do what you're supposed to do when you're supposed to do it, you will always encounter trials and tribulations you shouldn't have come across.

Magnification

The more strides you make, the more opportunities you have.

The more efforts you apply, the more rewards you reap.

The more challenges you encounter, the more abilities you develop.

The more stabilities you demonstrate, the more strengths you possess.

The more disciplines you establish, the more consistencies you experience.

The more confidence you display, the more advancement you ascertain.

The more you give, the more is given back to you in return.

The more strides you make, the more opportunities you have.

The more efforts you apply, the more rewards you reap.

The more challenges you encounter, the more abilities you develop.

The more stabilities you demonstrate, the more strengths you possess.

The more disciplines you establish, the more consistencies you experience.

The more confidence you display, the more advancement you ascertain.

The more you give, the more is given back to you.

It's hard to give your heart to a pessimist. She will never hold your hands to lead. Nor will she hold your hands to follow. She will, rather, drag you down into the pit of hell through her cynicism, through her condescension, through her inconsideration, through her skepticism, through her ignorance.

It's absolutely within our capabilities to love everyone around us selflessly. It's absolutely within our capabilities to care about everyone around us compassionately, affectionately, without reservation. It's most definitely within our capacities to bless everyone around us. Without exceptions, without discriminations, without condemnations.

Why Are You Running?

Why are you running?

Where are you going?

Why are you running?

Who are you running from?

Why so much of a hurry?

Why are you running?

Why so much in haste?

Why are you running?

Can't run past the gate of death.

Why are you running?

Who are you running from?

Why are you running?

Where are you running to?

Why so much of hurry?

Why so much in haste?

Where're you going?

Where're you coming from?

Where're you running to?

Can't run beyond the boundary of graveyard.

Why are you running?

Why are you so much of a hurry?

Why are you running?

Why are you so much in haste?

Why are you so much in desperation?

Who are you running from?

Can't run away from the challenges of life.

The people who ran faster yesterday,

Gone yet unnoticed.

The ones so much in a hurry,

Departed, buried before their time.

The ones who were so far ahead,

Forgotten without traces of their legacies.

People who were so far ahead

Sometimes missed all the fun.

People who were so far beyond

Sometimes missed all the jokes.

The people who ran too far ahead sometimes never took their time to see what they left behind.

It's not always about how much you have in your hands that defines or justifies your end result. It is always about what you do with it. You can have so much yet do so little. You can have so little yet do so much. It doesn't really matter how much you have in your hands. It's always about accomplishing the most with what you have that matters.

Sometimes in life we are just in too much of a hurry. Sometimes in life we are just so much in haste. Sometimes in life we are too impatient. Sometimes in life we are too self-contained, too self-absorbed, too close-minded. Instead to settle down to take a minute. Instead to settle down to take a second. Instead to settle down to rethink. Instead to settle down to recapture the moment, to understand the significance of right now before we rush out without capturing the importance of this moment without taking care of right now.

When we absolutely work on the positive methodologies, when we absolutely work on the progressive mechanisms, when we absolutely work on effective processes efficiently and consistently, we will realize that if the processes are right, the results are always the same.

The mind is a delicacy. Once fractured, it stays fractured. A fractured mind is a fragile mind, a brittle mind that needs care, that needs reforms, that needs rehabilitation, that needs compassion, that needs reassurance. A delicate mind is a confused mind that needs the reinforcement of love. That needs reengagement of attention. That needs rededication to care. That needs recognition of hidden potentials, of talents, of other peculiarities.

My Prideful Name

Names always precede

The owner of the name.

If you do good,

Your name shall drum awesomeness

Even before they call your name.

If you do great,

Your name

Shall drum excellence

Even before they see your face.

When they call you

A bad name

Out of ignorance

Even in your absence,

Shall have no semblance

To your fame.

Shall have no familiarity

To your good name.

Shall have no resemblance

To your prideful face.

Your name

Shall have no bearing

To those negative illusions.

Shall have no relevance

To those contaminations.

Shall have no recognition

To those condemnations.

Shall have no reception

To those abominations.

Yours is a good name.

A good name to have.

A good name to love.

A good name to admire.

A good name to protect.

A good name to be proud of.

When we fail to grow in life, we also fail to progress. When we fail to grow in life, we also fail to succeed. We fail to represent our true selves. We also fail to answer to our true callings. When we fail to grow in life, we also fail to realize our preordained dreams. We also fail to expand the scope of our perceptions. When we fail to grow in life, we also fail to reach our highest heights. We also fail everyone else in our circles.

Wish I Could Say Yes

Wish I could say yes when
supposed to say yes; wish I
could say no when
supposed to say no.

When I failed to make a left

When supposed to,

Or failed to make a right

When I should.

Destinies changed.

Couldn't be at the right place

I was supposed to be.

Couldn't hang with the right people

I was preordained to hang with.

Couldn't bless the right people

I was supposed to bless.

Couldn't love the people

I was supposed to love.

To say yes

When supposed to say yes.

To say no

When supposed to say no.

Progress would be made,

Destinies would be fulfilled.

A man has abilities to travel beyond the sphere of his own imperfection. Beyond his own misconceptions. Beyond his misadventures. Beyond his weaknesses. Beyond his unrealistic dreams. Beyond his fantasies. Beyond his ill-advised tendencies. He has the intrepidness, he has the tenacity to explore the intricacies of his own idiosyncrasies, of his own philosophies, of his own incertitude without guilt, without intimidations, without fear of the unknown. He is very comfortable with himself, very confident in his personality, in his wisdom, in his dexterity to be a leader of his own existence. To be a winner of his territory. To be a champion of his own people.

Can't be mad at yourself for who you are. Can't be disappointed in yourself for what you are. You can't be angry at the world for who you become. Can't blame humanity for the self-image you create. Can't disparage others for who they are. Can't kill yourself for the challenges you face. Be happy for who you are. Be happy for what you represent.

It's not just about our personal accolades. That matters as much as how positively we have impacted other people's lives around us with love. It's not just about our personal wealth. That matters as much. It's not just about our personal achievements. That matters as much. Not about our self-proclaimed arrogance. That matters as much as how positively we have improved other people's lives around us with kindness. Of how positively we have changed other people's lives with friendship, with the abundance of our blessings.

Our personal accomplishments are our own personal glory unless we use them to bless others without exemptions. Unless we use them to bless others without expectations. Unless we use them to bless others without condemnations. Without arrogance. It's all in vain. All for nothingness.

Don't be contemptuous. Don't be braggadocious. Don't be arrogant. This life is nothingness. The way we come is the same way we go back—emptiness, nakedness, nothingness.

Dynamism just doesn't come. Ordinarily. Not without sweat. Not without commitment. Not without efforts. Dynamism just doesn't come. Ordinarily. Not without performances. Not without sacrifices. Not without challenges. Dynamism just doesn't come. Ordinarily. Not without disappointments. Not without failures. Not without misfortunes.

I Am Who I Am

You are who you are;

I am who I am.

Your life is your life;

My life is my life.

You are who you are.

I am who I am.

Your fame is your pride.

My glory is my celebration.

Your success is your wealth.

My disappointment is my motivation.

Your time is your asset.

My day is my opportunity.

Your accomplishment is your victory.

My failure is my wisdom.

Your sadness is your sorrow.

My hardship is my strength.

Your dominance is your selfishness.

My redemption is in my destiny.

You are who you are.

I am who I am.

Your life is your life;

My life is my life.

You are who you are.

I am who I am.

Your high is your arrogance.

My low is my humility.

Your wickedness is your triumph.

My subservience is my pride.

My hope is my trust in God.

Sometimes in life it takes more than hard work to be successful against all odds. It takes more than relentlessness to be victorious. It takes more than perseverance to be triumphant. It takes more than a great personality to be self-accomplished against all odds.

Sometimes in life it takes more than self-righteousness to be above where others struggled to be victorious. Where others failed to be champions.

It takes more than ordinary commitments to make a big splash. It takes more than inconsistent efforts to make bigger strides. It takes more than mediocre performances to make impactful impressions. To revise generational failures. To revamp ungerminated dynasties. It takes more than lazy-mindedness to refine downtrodden cultures. To disown backward traditions. To rearrange failed practices. To replace unprogressive mannerisms. It takes more than guts to stand alone in the midst of a bigger crowd.

If you don't like something. change it instantaneously. Don't wait perpetually to change what you don't like about yourself. Don't wait forever to change what you don't like about the progressions of your journey. It may cost you your destiny. It may inadvertently restructure your preordained destinations. It may even cost you the actual topography of your lifestyle if you don't do something right now to change what you don't like about yourself. To change what you don't like about your lifestyle.

Time is Precious

Time is precious;

Time is significant.

Time is precious;

Time is relevant.

Time is very precious.

Time waits for nobody;

Time waits for no one.

Time waits for nobody;

Time waits for no one.

Time never waits for anybody.

Every minute is an opportunity.

Every day a game changer.

Every hour is a privilege.

Every day is a blessing,

Opportunity to reestablish,

Privilege to redirect,

Desire to progress,

Heart to love,

Mind to bless.

You are here today,

Gone tomorrow.

One minute

You're young,

Next second

You are old.

The day after,

You're gone.

Time is precious.

Time is very relevant.

Time is precious.

Time is very significant.

Time waits for no one.

You don't argue with the hands you are dealt. You ain't got control over it. You own it. You make it better. You make it the best ever.

People around you are your bread to greatness. People around you are your butter to your victories. When you take care of them, you've taken care of your progress. When you take care of them you've taken care of your success. You've taken care of your happiness.

When you're good, you can be better. When you're better you can be the best. When you are the best, you can be the greatest. When you are bad, you can be good. When you are average, there is still plenty of room for improvement.

A little blessing is a lot of blessing. One little blessing transforms life from nothingness to abundance.

Don't block your blessings. Nor should you block someone else's blessings through ignorance, through envy, through arrogance, through hatred from lack of wisdom.

A leader doesn't wait around to be told what to do. He is already doing it.

The future must be predictable for our efforts to be measurable. The future must be reassured for our performances to be rewarded according to our actions. According to our inactions.

When we elevate our minds to transcend normalcy, to dismantle the predictability of misfortunes, of misadventures, our lives will also be transformed beyond normalcy.

Ignorance is ignorance. It has no measurements. It has no calibrations. It has no surprises. It has no misunderstanding. When you're ignorant, you are ignorant.

Self-Preservation

Don't let ignorance define your destiny.

Don't allow fear determine your future.

Don't let hatred be the precursor of your attitude.

Don't allow misconceptions to preset your knowledge.

Don't let sentiment influence your character.

Don't allow misperceptions hinder your attributes.

Don't let superstitions impact your beliefs.

Don't allow unrefined traditions block your advancement.

Don't let selfishness deprive you of your blessings.

Don't allow ill-conceived doctrines to be the pinnacle of your existence.

Everybody is Not an Enemy

Everybody is not an enemy;

Everyone is not a friend.

Everybody is not for you;

Everyone is not against you.

Everybody is not your enemy;

Everyone is not your friend.

Everybody is not your lover.

When I open your heart,

I see hatred, envy, and malice,

Yet you're my best friend.

When y'all open my mind,

You see passion, admiration, and humility,

Yet you're my worst adversary.

When I fall on my knees,

Y'all refuse to lift me up.

Y'all run far away from me.

Yet y'all are my blood brothers.

When y'all are down on your luck,

I am right there, lifting y'all up.

Yet I don't even know your names.

Who you think you know,

You don't really know.

Who you think you see,

You don't really see.

Who you think you know,

You don't know at all.

You turn your back.

You see who you see.

You turn your sight.

You know who you see.

You turn your back.

You see your friends.

You turn your sight.

You see your enemies.

Everybody is not your enemy;

Everyone is not your friend.

Everyone is not for you;

Everybody is not against you.

Everyone is not your enemy;

Everybody is not your lover.

It's almost inconceivable for human beings to be so inconsiderate. Absolutely incomprehensible for human beings to be so selfish. To be so wicked. To be so untenable. Full of anger, full of hatred against each other. After all, we didn't bring anything in. We aren't taking anything out.

When our lives are more defined with positivism, when our futures are more predetermined with progressivism, when our personalities are more predictable with great expectations from an early age, there is always more clarity to our directions. There is always more certainty to our ambitions. There is always more reaffirmation to our goals. More reassurance to our expectations. There is always more focus to our destinations in life.

We have to care about each other. We have to show empathy to others. We have to show kindness to each other. We have to show love to one another. When we don't, humanity is for sale.

The future is only for the wise. The future is only for the strong. Only for the intellectuals. Only for the innovators. Only for the creators Of knowledge. Only for the innovators of integrity. Only for the creators of honors. The innovators of distinctions. Only for the creators of progressivism.

To be the best, you really have to work harder. To be great, you really have to work smarter. To be more successful, you really have to be more self-disciplined. To be more result-oriented. You really have to be more focused, be more attentive than everyone else around you.

Reformation doesn't come without sacrifices. Nor does immeasurable personal growth happen without misadventures, without failures.

Simplicity

Simplicity is beautiful.

Simplicity is awesome.

Simplicity is beautiful.

Simplicity is great.

Humility is not condescension.

Arrogance is demeaning.

Respect is not weakness.

Dexterity is opportunity.

Failure is not abomination.

Success is inspiration.

Leadership is not arrogance.

Friendship is admiration.

Personality is not confrontation.

Life is opportunity.

Living is blessing.

God, is supreme.

Simplicity is beautiful.

Simplicity is awesome.

Simplicity is great.

Simplicity is always beautiful.

No one is more special than another. No one is more superior than who you are when you consistently bring your absolute best. Even in the dark corridors, even in the open spaces. Even in the market squares. Through personal efforts, through genuine sacrifices, through excellent performances, without trepidations, without fear.

Excellent upbringing is everything in life. Great upbringing is a precursor to an outstanding commencement. To an electrifying personality. A catalyst to a beautiful lifestyle. To enviable mannerisms. An impetus to a magnificent future. To admirable accomplishments. To everlasting happiness.

Everyone needs someone else to hold his hands. At any given time, we all need someone to pump us up beyond mediocrity. Someone to uplift our souls beyond simplicity. Someone to elevate our mindsets above ineptitudes. Someone to uplift our emotions above failures.

Someone who always watches our backs. Who always watches our blind spots when no one else is watching.

You Have to Get Up

When you fall,

You have to get up.

When you fall,

You have to get up.

When you fall down,

You still have to get up.

Every time you fall,

You must get up.

Every time you fall down,

You must get yourself up.

Life is tough,

Full of challenges.

Life is hard,

Full of trials.

Life is difficult,

Full of tribulations.

Some easy to confront;

Some too rigid to approach.

Yet victories must be attained,

Yet battles must be won,

Yet progress must be made.

Failure is not an option.

Weakness is not a deterrent.

Dreams shall still be fulfilled.

Ambitions shall still be realized.

Destinies shall still be established.

God shall still be celebrated.

The beauty of our lives, the magnificence of our journeys are emblematic of our personal battles. They are symbolic of our own adversities. Of our misfortunes, of our struggles, of our inadequacies, of our triumphs, of our victories, our intelligence, our success, our personal stories.

They were the reflections, the fundamentals, the prognostications, the facades that captured our peculiarities. That transformed our personalities. That recalibrated our mannerisms. That reshaped our demeanors. That personalized our idiosyncrasies. They are the portraits of our escapades. The mirrors of our past transgressions. Of our endeavors, of our performances, of our accomplishments, of our upbringing, of our failures that never left our minds or departed from our memories. Even with the oblivion of time, they never go away.

Too many constraints, too many limitations, too many restrictions too much criticism, too much condemnation, too much discouragement are inimical to our self-growth. Inimical to our self-confidence. Inimical to our progress, to our success, to our victories, to our happiness.

You don't have to pull me down to be miserable with you. Rather, you should lift me up to enhance our opportunities to get us out of the shackles of miseries, out of. the shackles of poverty, out of the shackles of ignorance, out of the shackles of our downtroddenness.

it's cowardice to be quiet when we should be the loudest voices in the crowd of the ignoramuses, in the congregations of the dimwits. It may change the course of a life. It may reverse the plights of a community. It may even improve the progression of a society, or significantly transform the standing of a country when we all rise to instantaneously right the wrongs rather than to sit idly, doing nothing, expecting miracles from the above.

Right or Wrong

Life is about making right or wrong decisions.

Life is about making right or wrong decisions.

Life is about making right or wrong decisions.

It is always about making right or wrong decisions in life.

The decision to be ahead or to be behind.

The decision to be distinct or to be ordinary.

The decision to be proactive or to be negative.

The decision to be aggressive or to be tentative.

The decision to be assertive or to be timid.

The decision to be progressive or to be regressive.

The decision to be a blessing or to be a parasite.

The decision to be a leader or to be a follower.

The decision to be happy or to be miserable.

Life is about making right or wrong decisions.

Life is about making right or wrong decisions.

Life is about making right or wrong decisions.

It is always about making right or wrong decisions in life.

Change is hard. Change is difficult to attain. To make changes more effective, more relevant, more result-oriented, they have to come from within. They have to originate from our innermost, from our mindsets, from our perceptions. From our self-consciousness.

Change brings dynamic transformations that override the complexity of imperfection. It overturns the rigidity of criticisms. It overrides the reluctance to self-discipline. It overturns the lack of self-motivation to open-mindedness, to progressivism.

Change is attributable to our self-sacrifice. To our self-determination, to our self-preservation, to our self-orientation.

Change brings positive outcomes to our lives. Change brings great excitement to our visions. Change brings optimism to our self-motivation. Change brings resurgence to our perceptions. Change brings reinforcements to our self-preservation.

Change is good. A positive change is great. A little change here, a little change there will ultimately take us from the depth of the valley to the mountaintops.

Who Are Mine without You?

Who are mine without you, O Lord?

Who are mine without you, my Lord?

Who are mine without you, my Savior?

Who are mine without you, Olodumare?

Who are mine without your love?

Who are mine without your affection?

Who are mine without your grace?

Who are mine without your mercy?

Who are mine without your benevolence?

Who are mine without your salvation?

Who are mine without your favors?

Who are mine without your anointings?

Who are mine without you, O Lord?

Who are mine without Babaloke?

Who are mine without you, my Lord?

Who are mine without you, Olodumare?

Without you, Lord, I am a soul without a spirit.

Without you, Lord, I am a journey without a compass.

Without you, Lord, I am a tree without a root.

With you, Lord, in my life, I am a winner.

With you, Lord, in my life, I am a champion.

I am a prince of my universe.

Decision-making is one of the most important functions in human progressions in life. It's the key, the opium to our individualism, to our miracles, to our uniqueness, to our creativity, to our interconnectivities. It's the fountain of human advancements. It's the fountain of our progressiveness. It's the fountain of our ingenuity.

It defines the calibrations of our successes, of our commitments. It defines the measurements of our failures. It's instrumental to our personality traits, to our ideological impressions, to our assimilations, to our self-representations.

When a decision is positive, the impact, goes beyond ordinariness. The effect transcends expectations. When a decision is retrogressive, the damage also lasts for decades. The aftereffects last forever.

The mind is too powerful to be wasted on trivialities. The mind is too precious to be wasted on misconceptions. The mind is too powerful to be wasted on sentimentalities. The mind is too precious to be wasted on hatred. The mind is too beautiful to be wasted on inconsiderations.

Self-worth, through self-education, is absolutely essential to our personal growth.

Self-worth, through self-orientation, is very important to our self-confidence. Self-worth, through self-preservation, is very vital to our self-esteem, a necessity to our success, an urgency to our advancement, important components to our self-esteem. An enigma to our self-identity.

The more we invest in ourselves, the more structured our lifestyles also become. The more predictable our personal victories, the more result-oriented our success will also become.

We have to be cognizant of our own weaknesses in order for us to be able to tolerate other people's imperfections. We have to be self-aware of our own strengths in order for us to be patient enough to understand their inadequacies, in order for us to tolerate their inconveniences, in order for us to accept their failures.

Who Will Love Me?

Who will love me

If you don't?

Who will care for me

When you don't?

Who will lift me up

If you don't?

Who will be there for
me when you're not?

When I hold your hands,

My heart overjoys.

When you hold my hands,

My mind explodes with happiness.

When we hold each other's hand

My heart collapses with gratitude.

When I kiss your lips,

My life is never the same.

When you say you love me,
my heart stops breathing.

Don't leave me

Because you can.

I will not leave you

Because I can.

Don't run away from me

Because you can.

I will not run away from you

Because I can.

Don't leave me, babe,

Because you can.

I will never leave you, even if I can.

Who will love me if you don't?

Who will care for
me when you
don't?

Who will lift me up if
you don't?

Who will love me, babe,
when you don't?

Life is beautiful when you have it. Life is more fun when you're happy about your today. Life is more electrifying when you are elated about your tomorrow. Life is more exhilarating when you have good friends. Life is more beautiful when you have great families, when you have awesome people around you who lifts your spirits, who elevate your emotions to eternity … into utopianism … to heaven.

Opportunity is only accorded those who seek it, to those who look for it. When you are persistently knocking on its doors. it's just a matter of time before someone lets you in.

This is your heaven. You're already in it when you are consistently doing the right things. According to the dictations of your beautiful mindset, you are absolutely in it.

Sunshine

Why would you stay in the dark,

How could you stay in the dark,

Why should you stay in the dark,

How could you stay in the dark,

Why would you stay in the dark

When you could be in the light and shine?

When you could be in the light and jubilate?

When you could be in the light and celebrate?

When you could be in the light and rejoice,

Why would you stay in the dark,

Where there is evil and bad intention,

Where there is ignorance and condescension,

Where there is confusion and dissolution,

Where there is hatred and despondency,

Where there is envy and jealousy,

Where there is no vision nor future,

Where there is no love or friendship,

Where there is no beginning or end?

Why would you stay in the dark

When you could be in the light and shine,

When you could be in the light and jubilate,

When you could be in the light and celebrate?

The law of humanity stipulates that every life we touch, everybody we meet, every task we engage in, every activity we perform on our journeys should be a blessing to ourselves. Should be a comfort to others around us.

It's always the people around us who make our lives to be truly blessed. It's always the people around us who make our existence more meaningful, more exciting, more colorful.

You can't be half good or half righteous or half bad. Uprightness, righteousness, being good are about consistency. It is about being good, being righteous, being upright all the time. Anything contrary or in between is a heresy, a contradiction, a fake, a fraud, unorthodox, a heterodoxy.

Nothing Goes for Nothing

Nothing goes for nothing.

Nothing goes for nothing.

Nothing goes for nothing.

Have to sacrifice something for something.

Have to sacrifice hatred for love.

Have to sacrifice poverty for abundance.

Have to sacrifice frustrations for courage.

Have to sacrifice animosity for friendship.

Have to sacrifice arrogance for humility.

Have to sacrifice depression for happiness.

Have to sacrifice disruption for normalcy.

Have to sacrifice ineptitude for proactiveness.

Have to sacrifice mediocrity for distinctions.

Have to sacrifice ignorance for enlightenment.

Have to sacrifice stress for vibrancy.

Have to sacrifice complacency for self-actualization.

Have to sacrifice evil for godliness.

Life is about making the right sacrifices.

Life without challenges and expectancies is boring. Life without adversities and misadventures is abnormal. Life without fantasies, dreams, and celebrations is uneventful.

There is nothing wrong with addictions. We just have to be addicted to the positive things.

There is nothing wrong with obsessions. We just have to be obsessed with the right methods.

We just have to be more passionate about hard work. We have to be more consumed with integrity. We have to be more committed to honesty, more dedicated to uprightness, more dependent on progressivism.

It's not over. Not until it is over. Never over, not until you decide it is over. Don't give up on yourself. Don't give up on your dreams. Don't give up on your goals. Don't give up on your tomorrow. Don't give up on your future. Don't ever give up on your life.

Commencement

It's a new day; it's a new beginning. Today is a new day.

Today is my new beginning.

Today just begins.

Yesterday is gone.

Gone are sadness and depression.

Gone are stress and frustrations.

Gone are failure and bad luck.

Gone are regret and complaint.

Gone are ignorance and incompetence.

It's a new day—

A day of anticipations,

A day of exaltations,

A day of mercy,

A day of favors,

A day of anointings,

A day of blessings.

It's a new day—

A day of advancements,

A day of resources,

A day of recognition,

A day of excitement,

A day of joy,

A day of celebrations.

It's a new day; it's a new beginning.

Today is a new day.

Today is my new beginning.

Light is a powerful force over darkness. When it refuses to shine, when it refuses. to illuminate, when it refuses to brighten the darkness, forever remains the same—rigid, impenetrable, unapproachable, difficult to penetrate. Just like ignorance over knowledge. Just like stupidity over intelligence.

Friendship is an exchange. You care for me, I care for you. I do for you, you do for me. Otherwise, it's a waste of time.

Everything is in the open. Nothing is hidden. Everything is in the open. Nobody is invincible. Stop hiding yourself from yourself. Stop hiding yourself from others. Stop hiding yourself from the world.

A great mind has the capability to redirect its course. A great mind has the capacity to improve its focus. A great mind has the brilliance to restructure its direction. It has the ability to redirect its attention.

Ignorance

Don't look at me

And think

You know my name.

Don't look at me

And think

You see my heart.

Don't look at me

And think

You know my name.

Don't look at me

And think

You see my mind.

Not everyone

Who walks my way

Crosses my path.

Not everyone

Who crosses my path

Walks my way.

Not everyone

Who walks my way

Takes enough time

To know my name.

Not everyone

Who crosses my path is

Patient enough

To see my face.

Not everyone

Who walks my way is

Kind enough

To remember my name,

Sincere enough

To look my way,

Care enough

To hold my hand,

Patient enough

To know my mind,

Kind enough

To treat me the same.

Don't look at me

And think

You know my name.

Don't look at me

And think

You see my heart.

Don't look at me

And think

You know my name.

Don't look at me

And think

You see my mind.

When life is too easy, when life is too smooth, when life is too passive, something is terribly wrong. Life should be full of challenges, full of adversities, full of excitement, full of misadventures, full of optimism to make life more worthy of living.

The more ups we have in our lives, the more downs we have in our existence. The more accreditations we also have. The more practical solutions and the more wisdom we also possess along the way against unanticipated adversities, against unforeseeable complications, and against unwarranted tribulations.

Life brings challenges. Challenges bring excitement and optimism. Adversity brings triumphs and impactful leadership.

Anticipation

Don't wait;

Just proceed.

Don't walk;

Just run.

Don't run;

Just fly.

Don't crawl;

Just walk.

If you proceed when to wait,

Run when to walk,

Fly when to run,

Walk when to crawl,

You've already defined your destiny.

You've already made your impact.

You've already made your mark.

You've already made your name.

You've already established your future.

Don't wait; just proceed.

Don't walk; just run.

Don't run; just fly.

Don't crawl; just walk.

If you proceed when to wait,

Run when to walk,

Fly when to run,

Walk when to crawl,

You've already defined your destiny.

You've already made your impact.

You've already made your mark.

You've already made your name.

You've already established your future.

Our Mindset

It's all in the mind.

It's all in the mind.

It's all in the mind.

It's all in your mind.

Your mind either makes you or breaks you.

Your mind either lifts you up or brings you down.

Your mind that elevates you also denigrates you.

Your mind that advances you also self-deprecates you.

Your mind that motivates you also discourages you.

Your mind that compliments you also beats you down.

It's all in the mind.

It's all in the mind.

It's all in the mind.

It's all in your mind.

Your mind that sees your beauty also sees your ugliness.

Your mind that empowers you also sees your vulnerability.

Your mind that takes you higher will also drop you yonder.

Your mind that promotes your confidence also encourages your timidity.

Your mind that sets you up for success also set you up for failure.

Your mind either makes you or breaks you.

Self-Confidence

Self-confidence is not arrogance.

Ability is not over-confidence.

Distinction is not abnormality.

Success is not a stranger.

Accomplishment is not extraordinary.

Beauty is simplicity.

Love is humanity.

Humanity is love.

Friendship is compassion.

Leadership is uniqueness.

Ordinariness is humility.

Simplicity is admiration.

Personality is self-identity.

Self-confidence is not arrogance.

Ability is not over-confidence.

Distinction is not abnormality.

Success is not a peculiarity.

Accomplishment is not anomalous.

Life is Worthy of Living

Life is worth living

When you love yourself.

Life has more value

When you have ambitions.

Life is more exciting

When you believe in your abilities.

Life is more rewarding

When you set realistic goals.

Life is more fruitful

When you invest in your dreams and aspirations.

Life is worth living

When you love yourself.

Life is more reassuring

When you have self-confidence.

Life is admirable when you accept challenges.

Life is more gratifying

When you are result-oriented.

Life is more meaningful

When you are self-accomplishable.

Life is more predictable

When you have directions and self-discipline.

Optimism

Every day is a good day

When God is on your side.

Every day is a great day

When God is on your side.

Every day is a very good day

When God is on our sides.

It's a very good day

When you get up

In good health,

With a sound mind.

It's a very good day

When you are alive,

Among the living.

It's a very good day

When you have goals

To accomplish,

When you have visions

To actualize.

Every day is a very good day indeed

When you have victories

To celebrate.

When you give people what they want, they will also give you back more than what you need. Give them your heart. They will give you back more than their lives.

Upliftment

Your strength is my strength.

My weakness is your weakness.

Your strength is my weakness.

My weakness is your strength.

Your failure is my sadness.

My success is your triumph.

When you fall, I lift you up.

When I slip, you raise me up.

When you are down, I comfort you.

When I am up, you are up with me.

When you fall, I lift you up.

When I rise, you rise with me.

When you cry, I cry with you.

When I laugh, you laugh with me.

When you lead, I follow your lead.

When I err, you forgive me.

You are my brother.

I am your brother.

You are my brother.

I am your brother.

We are all family.

Humanity's endeavors have no limitations or restrictions. Humanity's performances have no constraints or impediments. Human progressions have no endings or beginnings. Empower your mind with big dreams. Empower your mind with unimaginably creative perceptions. Empower your mind with great visions without any boundaries, without any intimidation.

We all can't be wrong at the same time. But we all can be right at the same time.

When we are all on the same positive side of the coin, we have more positive progressions. We have more great momentums. We have more excellent outcomes in all our undertakings.

Don't be too complacent about your imperfections. Don't be too complacent with your weaknesses. Don't be too complacent about your inadequacies. Do something about them. Make the right changes, make the right decisions right now. Before it's too late.

It's the man who walks behind you who sees your behind. He is in a better position to see you from your blind spots. Don't be ignorant to criticism. Don't turn a stiff neck to good advice. That's the only way to make up for your imperfections. That's the only way to make up for your inadequacies, for your past mistakes.

Sometimes you get blindsided by the things that are beyond your self-control, that are beyond your understanding due to lack of preparation, lack of knowledge, lack of exposure, lack, of intelligence, lack of wisdom.

Exceptionalism doesn't come without merits, not without personal sacrifices. When you're exceptionally blessed with great upsides, even your enemies will recognize your peculiarities. They will admire your distinctions. They will also applaud your success. They will celebrate your victories.

Ignorant Mind

An ignorant mind is a dangerous mind.

An ignorant mind is a dangerous mind.

An ignorant mind is a very dangerous mind.

A complex mind to predict,

A difficult mind to impress,

A deceptive mind to honor,

A cynical mind to respect,

A selfish mind to celebrate,

A negative mind to change,

A pessimistic mind to emulate,

A primitive mind to educate,

An ugly mind to glorify,

A dangerous mind to love,

A complicated mind to comprehend.

An ignorant mind is a dangerous mind.

An ignorant mind is a dangerous mind.

An ignorant mind is a dangerous mind.

An ignorant mind is a very dangerous mind to love.

Don't be deceived. A man's self-made enemy is no one but himself. He is constantly standing in his own way, refusing to oblige to the realism of changes. Nor is he willing to adapt to the right expectations, to the dynamics of the true phenomenon of life.

Let your stars shine brilliantly so that the world can see your magnificence. Put your distinctions on display unapologetically so that your uniqueness is always a source of blessings to others.

It doesn't matter who takes care of a problem as long as a problem is taken care of. It doesn't matter who leads as long as we have somebody to lead.

You must have gone through hell innumerable times to have the audacity to withstand fire. You must have gone through hell numerous times to have the courage to neutralize fire.

Eyes Never Lie

Eyes never lie.

Eyes never lie.

Eyes never lie.

Eyes will never lie.

What you see is what you see.

What you see is what you know.

What you know is what you understand.

What you understand is what you apply.

What you apply is what you represent.

What you represent is what you become.

What you become is what you actualize.

Eyes never lie.

Eyes never lie.

Eyes never lie.

Eyes will never lie.

What you see is what you know.

What you know is what you understand.

What you understand is what you apply.

What you apply is what you represent.

What you represent is what you become.

What you become is your legacy.

Eyes never lie.

Eyes never lie.

Eyes never lie.

Eyes will never lie.

Son, please know who you are. Be resolute against who you are not. Be firm against what outside forces, alien to your upbringing, are telling you. Be resolute against people foreign to your traditions, strange to your culture are telling you to do.

Life is a continuum. Life is ever progressive. Life is ever evolving. Life is everlasting. Within her majestic undertone—irrespective of excuses, irrespective of ignorance, irrespective of a lack of awareness—the continuum persists, like the flow of rivers. If you get it, you get it. If you don't, you don't. Life moves on. As it was in the beginning, so shall it be. Life evolves with you; life evolves without you. Life is a continuum. Life is ever evolving. Life is ever progressive. Life is everlasting.

To be ordinary takes less effort. To be a pedestrian takes less preparation. To be a failure takes less commitment. It takes less attentiveness, less endeavors. less performances. It takes less engagements, less proactiveness, less skill sets. It takes less passion, less ambitions, less sacrifices, less concentration to be a disappointment, to be a failure in life.

Open Your Eyes

Open your eyes so you can see.

Open your mind so you can cogitate.

Open your heart so you can appreciate.

Open your vision so you can perceive.

Open your brain so you can conceive.

Open your ability so you can grow.

Open your conscience so you can be honest.

Open your eyes so you can see.

Open your mind so you can think.

Open your heart so you can love.

Open your vision so you can dream.

Open your brain so you can develop.

Open your abilities so you can advance.

Open your conscience so you can be great.

Open your eyes so you can perceive.

Open your mind so you can grow.

Open your heart so you can conceive.

Open your vision so you can advance.

Open your brain so you can think.

Open your abilities so you can develop.

Open your conscience so you can be free.

A mind will always transform itself to find its own course when it's nurtured, trained, to be subservient, to be submissive to the positive voices of reasoning and follow the path of progressivism, the path of righteousness, the path of uprightness.

It's all about the languages of self-representation. It's all about the languages, self-interpretation. It takes one to know one, to understand the other. If you understand my language, you may be privileged to the codes of my subjective body languages, to my assertions, to my gestures. But when we lack common ground, compatibility may be far-fetched.

We can't be lazy-minded about our todays. We can't be lackadaisical about. our tomorrows. We can't be nonchalant about our destinies. We can't be ill prepared. We can't be unsure. We can't be unsettled. We can't be disdained. We can't be unpredictable.

Our destinations, our lives, our journeys are intertwined. They are inseparable. They're in our hands. Let's do something about it.

You Have to Love Life to Live It

You have to love life to live it.

You have to live life to love it.

You have to live life to love it.

You have to love life to live it.

You have to love life to appreciate it.

You have to live life to complement it.

You have to love life to anticipate it.

You have to live life to be crazy about it.

You have to love life to dream about it.

You have to love life to enjoy it.

You have to live life to sacrifice for it.

You have to love life to believe in it.

You have to live life to commit to it.

You have to love life to die for it.

You have to love life to live it.

You have to live life to love it.

You have to live life to love it.

You have to love life to live in it.

The best qualities of our lives are predicated on the decisions, on the choices we make.

The choices, the decisions we make along the way will ultimately define the measurements of our personal accomplishments, will ultimately define the degree of our success. They are our lives; we should be in total control of our decisions. We should be in total control of our choices.

Sometimes in life we are just too much in a hurry. Too much in a haste. Sometimes in life we are just too impatient, too self-centered, too close-minded to settle down, to take a minute, to take a second to settle down, to think, to capture the moment, to understand the significance of right now before we rushed out, before we jumped up without crawling. When we absolutely trekked on, walked on, engaged in the positive functions in the progressive mechanisms, in the right process, effectively, efficiently, consistently. We will then realize that if the processes are right, the results are always the same.

This is my world. This is my life. When you are in it, you are relevant. When you are not in it, you don't matter. You are a nonentity.

Success is like liquor—powerful, intoxicating, addictive. Once tasted, you are addicted for life.

When you give people what they want, they will give you back more than what you need. Give them humility, and they will pay you. back with kindness. Give them kindness, and they will give you back their hearts. Give them your love, and they will give you back more than their lives.

Can't Be Hesitant

Can't be hesitant about your future.

Can't be ambiguous about realities.

Can't be ignorant about knowledge.

Can't be nonchalant about your attitudes.

Can't be inattentive about your commitments.

Can't be negligent about responsibilities.

Can't be disillusioned about challenges.

Can't be discouraged about your aspirations.

Can't be uninformed about resilience.

Can't be uncompassionate about humanity.

Can't be hesitant about your future.

Can't be ambiguous about realities.

Can't be ignorant about intelligence.

Can't be nonchalant about your attitudes.

Mediocrity is a curse. Lack of intelligence is a deprivation, an anomaly. We're absolutely shortchanged in the realities of life, deprived of the best of our existence when we settle for little, when we settle for nothing because of lack of effort, lack of preparation, lack of performance.

Life is daily. Every day is relevant. Today is just as important as yesterday. Yesterday was just as essential as tomorrow. Your deeds today will justify your reactions tomorrow, just like your deeds yesterday justified your conditions today. Think about it. A positive attitude always triumphs over negative reactions today, yesterday, tomorrow.

Don't be deceived. A man's self-made enemy is no one but himself. He is constantly standing in his own ways, refuses to oblige to the realism of changes, unwilling to submit to the true. phenomenon. Unwilling to submit to the true dynamics of life's expectations and realism.

When you are good, you are good for yourself. When you are bad, you are also being bad to yourself. It's always about you being good or being bad to yourself or for yourself. It always comes back to you being good or being bad.

No Pain, No Gain

No pain, no gain.

No pain, no gain.

No pain, no gain.

No life without desires.

No future without goals.

No triumphs without endeavors.

No wisdom without tribulations.

No success without sacrifices.

No strengths without abilities.

No excitement without enthusiasm.

No victory without triumphs.

No rehabilitation without collapse.

No celebration without victories.

No God without humanity.

No humanity without God.

Use your mind positively to complement your life. Take advantage of your thought process to advance your tomorrow. We all have choices. We all have hopes. We all have concentration. We all have obligations to be better than yesterday, to be greater than today.

Everybody aspires to greatness, but only few get to that pinnacle of exaltation through genuine efforts, through self-interests, through personal involvement.

The mind does grow. Give it some positive nutrients, and it will grow exponentially beautiful and magnificently impressive.

Life without challenges is boring. Life without expectancy is uninteresting. Life without adversities is abnormal. Life without misadventure is monotonous.

Triviality

Life is vanity.

Life is triviality.

Life is vanity.

Life is triviality.

Life is triviality.

Life is vanity.

You come, you go.

You up, you down.

You win, you lose.

You high, you low.

You hot, you cold.

You happy, you sad.

You laugh, you cry.

You rich, you poor.

You strong, you weak.

You sick, you strong.

You young, you old.

You live, you die.

Life is vanity.

Life is triviality.

Life is triviality.

Life is vanity.

Life is beautiful when you have it. Life is even more beautiful when you have someone special in it with you.

A little bit of wickedness, a little bit of selfishness displayed always overshadowed all the goodness, all the kindness expressed.

Ignorance is ignorance. It has no measurements; it has no calibrations. When you are ignorant, you are ignorant.

You can't win a battle in a second. You can't win a war in a minute. It takes a lifetime of preparation, hard work, consistency, reliabilities, dexterity, and diligence to win the battles of life, to overcome the devastating challenges of our lives to overcome the overwhelming tribulations of our existence.

Mentorship is very essential to our own personal growth. Everyone needs someone to help to navigate him or her against what he or she doesn't know against what he or she doesn't see against what he or she. doesn't understand.

Credibility is reliability. Reliability is consistency. When you are reliable, you are credible. When you are credible, you are also very consistent.

Personality is distinctiveness. If you ain't got it, you ain't got nothing special. You're just one of the commoners.

Son, don't be deceived by a fake soothsayer who says your destiny is in anyone else's hand but your own.

It takes someone special—a champion, a leader—to see what's wrong and make it right instantaneously, without hesitation, without trepidation, without fear.

The race doesn't stop at the starting point. It actually ends at the finishing line. Don't give up on yourself. Don't give up on your today. Don't give up on your tomorrow. Don't give up on your future.

Fear of failure shouldn't preclude us from the willingness to make efforts to succeed. Nor from the expressions, the audacity to challenge the intimidation of failures.

Through our beliefs, through hard work, through our skill sets, through our knowledge, through display of our intelligence, through display of our commitments, through display of our personal sacrifices to be above the water, irrespective of the conditions, irrespective of our situations. A man has to be a man. A man has to be self-conscious. He has to be self-confident of his representations. He has to be self-aware of his abilities to succeed at all costs.

It's against the divine nature of humanity to be someone other than yourself. There is only one you. Be yourself, be unique, be special, be distinct without any apology to anybody but yourself.

Humanism

Nobody is a slave.

Nobody is a king.

Nobody is rich.

Nobody is poor.

Nobody is a servant.

Nobody is a master.

Nobody is righteous.

Nobody is a sinner.

Nobody is perfect.

Nobody is imperfect.

Nobody is an enemy.

Nobody is a friend.

We are all the same

With the same mindsets,

With the same feelings,

With the same visions.

We are all the same

With the same perceptions,

With the same expectations.

Nobody is a loser.

Nobody is a winner.

We are all humanity.

We are all humans beings.

We are all the same.

Power is in the mind. Whatever our minds dwell on, believe in, concentrate on, act upon always comes to fruition, always comes to reality.

Nobody has it all. Nobody knows it all. You don't have to know it all, you don't have to have it all to be a blessing to yourself and to be a blessing to others around you.

Think before you act for every action has a reaction. And every reaction has consequences and implications.

Integrity is not just a virtue. It's the only prerequisite that defines the true nature of humanity. You've got to have it, or you are subhuman.

The brother standing next to you is your brother. Hold on to his hands. Nurture him with love. Bless him with care. Encourage him with friendship. The payback is enormous.

It takes wisdom. It takes temerity, it takes self-discipline to see the light when everyone else convincingly believe that darkness is the light.

Humanity should be above superficiality. Human beings should be above wickedness. We should be above hatred. We should be above jealousy. We should be above evil-mindedness. We should be above abnormalities. We're all the same, beautifully made with a perfectly sound mind of God.

A great upbringing is everything in life. An excellent upbringing is a precursor to an awesome commencement, a preamble to an excellent lifestyle. Good upbringing is a catalyst to a progressive beginning, a stimulant to an exciting future.

You have to ride with the wise in order to be wiser. You have to hang with the intellectuals in order to be measurable. In order to be celebrated. like an intelligentsia.

Stagnancy

Standing on the corner,

Standing on the same corner,

Standing on that same corner,

Doing the same thing

Over and over again.

Doing the same thing

Over and over again.

Still lives in the same house,

Still hangs with the same crowd,

Still hangs with the same friends.

Still has the same dreams,

Still aspires to the same goals,

Still makes the same mistakes.

Have to get out of this corner,

Have to get out of this place.

Have to get out of this same corner.

Minutes had turned to hours.

Hours had turned to days.

Days had turned to weeks.

Weeks had turned to months.

Months had turned to years

Still standing on that same corner.

Still standing on the same principles,

Still standing on the same beliefs,

Still standing on the same expectations.

Still standing on that same corner,

Corner of ignorance and backwardness,

Corner of fantasies and disillusions,

Corner of hatreds and prejudices,

Corner of frustrations and despondency,

Corner of doubts and procrastinations,

Corner of misrepresentations and hopelessness.

Have to change my ways.

Have to change my thinking.

Have to change my associations.

Have to change my perceptions.

Have to change my motivations.

Have to change my engagements.

Have to change my perspectives.

Have to change my consciousness.

Have to change my perspectives.

Have to change my habits.

Have to reposition myself.

Have to get out of this corner.

You can't just settle for ordinariness. You can't just settle for poverty. You can't just be content with failure, with depression, with melancholy, with futility, with ineptitude. You just can't accept mediocrity. Can't just accept incompetence. Can't just accept ignorance. Can't just accept close-mindedness. Can't just accept hatred. Can't just accept low self-esteem. Can't just accept lack of self-motivation to set the pace as the cornerstones of your life, as the navigator of your lifestyles. That's not you, not your destiny, not who you are. You're created to be a warrior. You're created to be a champion with self-pride, with honors, with distinctions, with integrity, with a beautiful mindset.

Don't do it. Not just because someone else. is doing it if it doesn't have any relevance to your progression in life. If it doesn't have any meaning to the betterment of your future, then stop, rethink, refresh, reapproach.

When you give people what they want, they will give you back more than what you need. Give them your heart. They will give you back more than their lives.

Pretentiousness

Uniqueness is not unique when
it's not demonstrated.
Distinction is not impactful
when it's not visible.

Love is not significant when it's
compromised.

Opportunity is a privilege when it is
selectively apportioned.

Happiness is far-fetched when there
is fear and tribulation.

Humanity is not humane when there
is prejudice and bigotry.

Life is not completely fulfilled when
it's not lived to its full potentiality.

Freedom is not completely free

When there are constraints and limitations.

We have to keep moving. We can't get stuck in one place. We can't get stuck in one situation. We can't get stuck with one belief. We can't get stuck with one ideology. Not with one doctrine. Nor with one concentration. Not with one dominion. Not with one culture. Nor with one tradition. We have to keep moving, refreshing our mentalities, expanding our mindsets, extending our horizons with positive thinking, with progressive mindsets till we change the world for the better.

Interconnectivity

Every action has a reaction.

Every link has its own directions.

Every action has a direction.

Every reaction has its own implications.

Every decision has its consequences.

Every possibility has its own challenges.

Every obstacle has its solutions.

Every tribulation has its own opportunities.

Every trial has its own credibility.

Every battle has its own triumphs.

Every situation has its own dynamics.

Every problem has its own rewards.

Every life has its own distinct predestinations.

Every action has a reaction.

Every link has its own directions.

Every action has its own significance.

Every reaction has its own implications.

You have to take care of yourself. If you don't, nobody else will. You have to assert your destiny through demonstrations of courage, through great visions, through awesome perceptions, through self-discipline, through resiliency. Your life is your life. It's in your total control. Whatever you do with it is your own business.

Life is not boring. Life is vibrant. Life is not stagnant. Life is lively. Life is ever evolving. Life is ever progressing. When you're stuck in life at any given time, you have to seriously reassess your motivations. You have to reevaluate your situations. You have to redetermine your positions. You have to reaffirm your beliefs. You have to revamp your commitments.

When a sacrifice isn't worth its salt, it isn't worthwhile. When a sacrifice isn't worth its salt, move on to better things. Time is too precious. It shouldn't be wasted on unrewarded sacrifices.

Great Leaders are Hard to Find

Great leaders are hard to find,

Noblemen harder to come across.

Conscience has been lost to selfishness.

Love has been stomped for hatred.

Humility has been trampled for arrogance.

Beauty has been subjected to ugliness.

Humanity condescended to barbarism.

God has been relegated to humanity.

Lives wasted for intolerance.

Potentials neglected because of racism.

Talents subjugated because of colors.

Commonality emerged as a celebrity.

Insensitivity has become weapon of destruction.

Distinctions are hard to recognize.

Great leaders are hard to find.

Noblemen harder to come across.

Unique leaders harder to come across.

Intelligence is the ace in the games of life. When you don't have it, you've already lost the game.

When you don't love yourself, when you don't appreciate your potential, you will never love others. You will never appreciate their efforts. You will never appreciate their performances either.

It's really hard to find yourself when you don't know who you are. Much harder to find happiness, much harder to find self-fulfillment when you don't have any clue about yourself. When you don't have any idea about your self-representations.

A Man without Honor

A man without honor is a man without integrity.

A man without humility is a man without pride.

A man without vision is a man without perception.

A man without goals is a man without selfish ulterior motives.

A man without wisdom is a man without enlightenment.

A man without dreams is a man without excitement.

A man without knowledge is a man without a future.

A man without direction is a man without ambition.

A man without self-identity is a man without representations.

A man without honor is a man without integrity.

A man without a conscience is a man without God.

A man without honor is a man without respect.

A man without humility is a man without honor.

A man without a vision is a man without future.

A man without goals is a man without self-motivation.

You have it wrong once. You have it wrong too many times. In the journey of life, you can't afford to have it wrong too many times.

Prestige and accolades only belong to those who deserve them, not necessarily because of age, not necessarily because of positions, not because of status, not because of affinity, but because of outstanding displays of integrity, of selflessness, of intelligence, of uprightness.

It's a herculean task to impact a foolish mind with knowledge. His mind is already preoccupied with his own misconceptions, clouded by his ignorance, blindfolded by his imbecility, by his reluctance to listen to the voice of reason.

Don't worry about your enemies or be perturbed about what they are saying behind your back. Let their hatred their antagonism their critiques motivate you to the brim of your personal growth, to the pinnacle of your victory and success.

Can't be afraid. of humanity. You are one of us. Can't be scared of death. It comes when it comes Can't be tired of living. That's the only reason you are here. Life is sweet. Life is bitter. Life is magnificent. Life is a challenge. It doesn't last forever. Enjoy it now, while you are here.

Ascension

Need to get up.

Need to rise up.

Need to stand up.

Need to get out—

Get out of my funks,

Get out of my situations,

Get out of my frustrations,

Get out of my depressions,

Get out of my unhappiness,

Get out of my hopelessness.

Need to stand up again.

Need to get out of the way.

Need to get up again.

Need to stand up again—

Stand up for me,

Stand up for myself,

Stand up for my visions,

Stand up for my goals,

Stand up for my beliefs.

Just have to rise up.

Just have to get up.

Just have to get out,

Out of my funks again.

Your life has only the definition you give it. Your life has only the representations you give it. You can either give it distinctive representations and enjoy the high that comes along with it. Or you can give it negative, downward representations and enjoy the lows that also go along with it. It's always about your personal decisions. It's always about your personal choices. It's either that you are on the right side or on the wrong side of the coin. You can't be on both sides at the same time.

Consistency is a beautiful attribute of greatness in humanity. To have. A good name to bear, a magnificent brand to wear. When you are good. Always be good. When you are good, be excellently good so that when your name is called, they already know your peculiarities, they already know your distinctions, they already know your character. They already know your name and your stories.

Change is Good

Change is good.

Change is great.

Change is good.

Change is awesome.

Change is human.

Change is inspiration.

Change is discipline.

Change is challenge.

Change is difficult.

Change is sacrifice.

Change is courage.

Change is positive.

Change is progress.

Change is happiness.

Change is leadership.

Change is a necessity.

Life is an open space. It is infinity. It has no beginning; it has no end. It has no sorrow; it has no joy. It has no sympathy; it has no triumph. It has no love; it has no sadness. It has no prejudice; it has no enemy. It has no bias; it has no favors. When you are here, it's here with you. When you are not here, it goes on without missing you.

Life is all about people. People are about life. The more people you have in your life, the more evolving, the more vibrant, the more exciting your life becomes.

Life is Not a Joke

Life is not a joke.

Life is not a joke.

Life is not a joke.

Every day is significant.

Every day is important.

Every day is significant.

Every day is an opportunity.

Have to be the best I can be.

Have to reestablish my destiny.

Have to reset my goals.

Have to love myself.

Have to have compassion for others.

Have to set a road map to my destinations.

Have to have strong beliefs in my abilities.

Have to demonstrate courage to promote my distinctions.

Life is not a joke.

Life is not a joke.

Every day is significant.

Every day is important.

Every day is an opportunity.

To Be a Winner

To be majestic, you have to hang with the elites.

To be a winner, you have to hang with the champions.

To be exceptional, you have to hang with the intellectuals.

To be principled, you have to hang with the winners.

To be spiritual, you have to hang with the righteous.

To be intelligent, you have to hang with the intelligentsia.

To be successful, you have to hang with the great achievers.

To be triumphant, you have to hang with the accomplishers.

To be victorious, you have to hang with God.

To be majestic, you have to hang with the kings.

To be a winner, you have to hang with the intellectuals.

To be exceptional, you have to hang with the elites.

To be principled, you have to hang with the champions.

To be spiritual, you have to hang with the great achievers.

To be intelligent, you have to hang with the intelligentsia.

To be self-satisfied, you have to hang with the righteous.

To be triumphant, you have to hang with the accomplishers.

To be victorious, you have to hang with God and humanity.

Humanity has undeniable power over its destiny. It has absolute control over its choices, over its decisions, over its mannerisms. When humanity fails or errs, it is often not from lack of courage or from lack of visions to recognize the intricacies of its choices, of its decisions, of its expectations. Rather, it's the laziness of its mind that exposes humanity's weakness, vulnerability to its indecisiveness, to procrastination, to pretentiousness. To humanity's imperfections.

Emancipation

Emancipate yourself from yourself.

Emancipate your mind from your wrongness.

Emancipate your spirit from your craziness.

Emancipate your life from subjugations.

Emancipate yourself from your inadequacies.

Emancipate your mind from your ignorance.

Emancipate your spirits from inferiority complexes.

Emancipate yourself from your insensitivities.

Emancipate your mind from procrastinations.

Emancipate your spirit from low self-esteem.

Emancipate your destiny from becoming downtrodden.

Emancipate your conscience from wickedness.

Emancipate your personality from wrong impressions.

Emancipate your spirit from bitterness and regrets.

Show Me Your Face

Show me your face

So I know who you are.

Tell me your mind so

I know your heart.

Declare your motive so

I know your intentions.

Surrender your heart so

I know you are humble.

Display your personality so

I know your distinctions.

Exhibit your representations so

I know your self-identity.

Impress me with your dedication

So I know your commitments.

Communicate your ideologies

So I know your uniqueness.

Impact me with your principles so

I know your characters.

Audacity

Not afraid of the challenges of tomorrow.

Not traumatized by the expectations of today.

Not dismayed by the demand for a better future.

Not worried about my self-representations and beliefs.

Not troubled about my weaknesses and imperfections.

Not inspired by self-centeredness and bigotry.

Not constrained by condemnations and prejudices.

Not impressed with pretentiousness and arrogance.

Not surprised by my foresightedness and integrity.

Not overwhelmed by personal challenges and struggles.

Not disillusioned about my goals and milestones.

Not dismayed by the lack of success of my struggles.

Not traumatized by the challenges of tomorrow.

I am on the right path with humanity.

I am on the right path with God.

I am on the right path with God.

I am on the right path with humanity.

Procrastination is a symptom of laziness of the mind. When we refuse to do what we need to do at the time we're destined to do it, we lose momentum. We lose positive energy. We lose the right of the way to actuate our intentions.

Our destinies' tie to the timeline of our actions or inactions when we drag our feet. And when we are hesitant to be more proactive in making the right decisions within the timeframe of positive outcomes are interrelated to our destinies' progression. Our destinies change retrogressively forever.

No God without Humanity

No humanity without God.

No God without humanity.

No end without beginning.

No sorrow without misery.

No gain without pain.

No success without sacrifice.

No achievements without failures.

No friendships without hostilities.

No love without hatred.

No humanity without God.

No God without humanity.

No end without beginning.

No sorrow without misery.

Paradise

Kindness is blessing.

Friendship is compassion.

Relationship is opportunity.

Generosity is beneficence.

Bravery is courage.

Maturity is wisdom.

Success is confidence.

Compliment is empowerment.

Accomplishment is self-pride.

Happiness is self-satisfaction.

Joy is heaven.

Kindness is blessing.

People are wealth.

Family is a paradise.

Nothing Lasts Forever

Nothing lasts forever.

Bone grows old.

Body decays.

Knowledge fades.

Wisdom declines.

Health dwindles.

But legacy lives on.

Past deeds become relevant.

Present endeavors so significant.

Future engagements so crucial.

But legacy lives on.

Nothing lasts forever.

Nothing lasts forever.

Life is Today

Life is now.

Life is today.

Life is this minute.

Life is this second.

Life is right now.

When life is gone,

All is gone.

Opportunities lost forever.

When life is gone,

All is gone.

All lost in vain.

Life is now.

Life is today.

Life is this minute.

Life is this second.

Life is right now.

Uprightness

Leadership is not meant for the imbeciles.

Godliness is not the subject of the heartless.

Goodwill only for the conscientious.

Blessings to the givers.

Salvations for the believers.

Godliness is only for the righteous.

Leadership is not meant for the imbeciles.

Godliness is not the subject of the heartless.

Goodwill only for the conscientious.

Blessings to the givers.

Salvations for the believers.

Godliness is only for the righteous.

I Am a Champion

I am a champion.

I am a winner.

I am a leader.

I admire myself

Because I invest in my abilities.

I love myself

Because I believe in my goals.

I respect myself

Because I have great character.

I encourage myself

Because I have hopes.

I discipline myself

Because I have principles.

I push myself

Because I have ambitions.

I love my friends

Because I love myself.

I pray to God

Because I believe in salvation.

I am a champion,

I am a winner,

I am a leader,

And I admire my potentials.

My Complexion

Don't think I am stupid

Because of my color.

Don't think I am ignorant

Because of my complexion.

Don't think I am incompetent

Because of my distinctions.

Don't think I am a failure

Because of my pronouncements.

Don't think I am a follower

Because of my humility.

Don't think I am a weakling

Because of my representations.

Don't think my life is conclusive

Because of my situations.

Don't think I am stupid

Because of my color.

Don't think I am ignorant

Because of my complexion.

Don't think I am incompetent

Because of my inadequacies.

A man doesn't define a situation. Situations define a man. Put a man in a peculiar situation, and you'll find out exactly who he is.

We can't be half good. We can't be half upright. We can't be half righteous. Life is about being good, being righteous, being upright all the time.

It's not over. It's never over. Not until you decide it's over. Don't give up on yourself. Don't give up on your dreams. Don't give up on your tomorrow. Don't give up on your future. Don't ever give up on your life.

Exaltation

To be alive is beautiful.

To be blessed is unique.

To be distinct is awesome.

To be tolerant is commendable.

To be persistent is confidence.

To be consistent is discipline.

To be competitive is motivation.

To be principled is consistency.

To be successful is dedication.

To be cohesive is advancement.

To be happy is satisfaction.

To be a leader is courageous.

To be fair is wisdom.

If you're struggling to get to your destinations, don't stop. Don't quit. Don't get discouraged. Be focused; be disciplined. You will be there eventually. In fact, the longer it takes, the more fun, the more adventures, the more experiences, the more versatility, the more wisdom you earn. Along the way, the more friends you will make.

Life is beautiful when you have it. Life is even more fun when you're happy about your today. When you are elated about your tomorrow, life is electrifying. Life is exhilarating and more exciting when you have. good friends, when you have great families, when you have caring people around you who lift your spirits, lift emotions, and lift your souls to eternity.

Righteousness

A righteous man is

A man of virtue,

A man of simplicity,

A man of candor,

A man of distinction,

A man of self-fulfillment,

A man of consideration,

A man of the downtrodden.

A righteous man is

A man of valor,

A man with enviable characteristics,

A man of spiritual endowment,

A man of progressivism,

A man of positivism,

A man of compassion,

A man of the people,

A man with a clear conscience.

A righteous man is

The man of the people.

A righteous man is

The beauty of humanity.

A righteous man is

The replica of Almighty God.

Winners always win. Winners win irrespective of situations. Irrespective of conditions, winners never quit. Despite obstacles, winners never stop. In spite of challenges, winners never give up on themselves. They never give up on their dreams, on their aspirations. The wind may blow, the hurricane may hit, the earthquake may distort the topography of their destinies. But through self-reliance, through resiliency, through self-discipline, through indefatigability, they will ultimately find the right courses, find the right environments, the right platforms to accomplish their intentions. No excuses allowed, no apologies entertained, no self-doubts accepted, no self-pity encouraged. Winners will always win irrespective of hindrances, irrespective of complications, irrespective of setbacks. The tougher the challenges, the more memorable are the triumphs, and the more celebratory are the victories.

We can't be too cynical, we can't be too timid, we can't be too lackadaisical about our present conditions. Nor can we be too afraid about future challenges. We can't stop being inquisitive about the greatest aspect of the endowments of God in our lives. Nor shall we be too tentative about the natural blessings of the Almighty in our existence.

It's not how far we have come that matters as much as how well we have done. The imprints we have left, the lives we have blessed, and the legacies we have built define how far we have come, defines how well we have done.

When we say yes, we get things done. The more yeses we say, the more things we get accomplished.

The beauty of life is the power of self-representation, the cognizance of our self-identities to know who we are, to know what we are, to know where we are, to know where we are going. It's self-realization of our distinctions, of our uniqueness, of our sense of pride.

Divinity

Humanity is not a sacrilege.

Humanity is not a desecration.

Humanity is not an abomination.

Humanity is not a monstrosity.

Humanity is not an abnormality.

Humanity is not racism.

Humanity is sacredness.

Humanity is divinity.

Humanity is kindness.

Humanity is jubilation.

Humanity is positivism.

Humanity is opportunism.

Humanity is comradeship.

Humanity is compassion.

Humanity is love.

Humanity is life.

Humanity is beautiful.

Humanity is godliness.

It doesn't take all of us to change the world. It only takes one or two great leaders bold enough to set the pace to change our existence.

For a man to be greater than himself, he has to be self-conscious. He has to be self-aware of his strengths. He has to recognize his weaknesses. He has to understand his visions. He has to honor his sacrifice. He has to care about the people around him.

Your efforts are not as rewarding, your success not as gratifying when all your concentrations are solely on yourself. When only your ulterior motives are on your mind, without consideration for others.

The Good or the Evil?

The good or the evil?

The good who fears and obeys,

Who leads and excels,

Who cares and respects,

Who motivates and commends,

Who forgives and elevates,

Who blesses and sacrifices.

Or

The evil, who despises and loathes,

Who lies and betrays,

Who gossips and envies,

Who hates and discourages,

Who condemns and backbites,

Who subjugates and kills.

The good or the evil?

We have to be versatile. We have to be multifaceted. We have to be inclusive. We have to be open-minded to different ideologies, to different philosophies, to different methodologies, to different opinions, to progressive beliefs in order to build a distinctive self-representation to establish positive personality traits.

Life can be sweet. Life can be bitter. It all depends on individual situations. It all depends on individual lifestyles. Create your own paradise through self-initiative paradigm shifts to welcome joy, to invite peace, to welcome self-contentment, and to allow happiness into your life and into the lives of people. around you.

You have to feel it to believe it. You have to believe it to dream it. You definitely have to dream it to actuate it. Success is about feeling it. Success is about believing it. Success is about dreaming it. Success is about actualizing it.

Elevation

Happiness is the antidote to depression.

Humility is the precursor to self-esteem.

Friendship is the solution to animosity.

Dexterity is the remedy to mediocrity.

Ability is the solution to ineptitude.

Humility is the antidote to arrogance.

Activities is the solution to futility.

Success is the enemy of failure.

Proactiveness is the antidote to backwardness.

Kindness is the only solution to antagonism.

Humanitarianism is the remedy to barbarism.

Happiness is the antidote to depression.

Humility is the precursor to self-esteem.

Friendship is the solution to animosity.

Dexterity is the remedy to mediocrity.

Ability is the solution to ineptitude.

Bitterness doesn't elevate our spirits. It brings us down to a stagnation. When we are resentful about today. We get nothing done. When we are pessimistic about tomorrow, when we are cynical about the future, we get nothing accomplished. But when we are happy, elated, when we are optimistic, our spirits will be salivating for tomorrow's tasks, for tomorrow's events, for tomorrow's activities, for tomorrow's victories.

It's a good feeling to be loved by our peers. It's a great feeling to be adored by our friends, by our families. It's even more gratifying, more intoxicating. more appreciated when they celebrate us for who we are, for our sincerity, for our exemplary attitudes. for our positive impacts, open-mindedness, and progressive imprints in their lives, in their livelihoods, in their communities.

We all have to walk in unison in order for us to be more accomplished. We all have to walk in uniformity in order to be more formidable. We all have to walk together in order for us to be more powerful. We have to walk in unison to be more relevant, to be more disciplined, to be more results-oriented so that we can reach the climax of our progressions. So that we can reach the apex of our aspirations and the pinnacle of our advancements in life.

Intellectualism

Out of ignorance comes knowledge.

Out of foolishness comes wisdom.

Out of stupidity comes intelligence.

Out of hard work comes prosperity.

Out of confidence comes victory.

Out of kindness comes blessing.

Out of perception comes conception.

Out of humanity comes greatness.

Out of God comes humanity.

Out of ignorance comes wisdom

Out of foolishness comes intelligence.

Out of stupidity comes knowledge.

Out of hard work comes victory.

Out of confidence comes greatness.

Out of kindness comes blessing.

Out of perception comes conception.

Out of humanity comes prosperity.

Out of humanity comes God.

The mind is delicate. Once fractured, it stays fractured. A fractured mind is a fragile mind, a brittle mind that needs care, that needs reforms, that needs rehabilitation, compassion, and reassurance. A delicate mind is a confused mind that needs the reinforcement of love, that needs reengagement of attention, that needs rededication to care, that needs recognition of their hidden potential, that needs recognition of their talents, that needs recognition of their dexterity.

Each challenge comes with its own dynamics. Each dynamic comes with its own situations. Each situation comes with its own opportunities.

It has to be a constant education to impact a culture that has been denigrated. It has to be a constant reeducation to change a tradition that has been damaged or to influence a mind that has been neglected, that has been trampled on, that has been condescended upon, deceived, discouraged to be the most attractive among its peers.

Empowerment

To empower is to bless.

To lead is to establish.

To educate is to enlighten.

To embrace is to accept.

To persevere is to succeed.

To emulate is to compliment.

To appreciate is to celebrate.

To congregate is to rejoice.

To educate is to empower.

To love is to care.

To care is to love.

To love is to live.

To empower is to bless.

To lead is to establish.

To educate is to enlighten.

To embrace is to accept.

To persevere is to succeed.

To emulate is to compliment.

The most precious thing a man can ever possess is his life. Nothing else is as significant. Without his life, there is no man. There is no life, there is no us, there is no today, there is no tomorrow, there is no humanity. There is no God.

Your life is your life. it only belongs to you. It's in your hands, in your total control. Without it, nothing else matters. Without it, you are a nonentity. Take care of yourself. Take care of your life. That's all you ever have.

When the mind is messed up, everything else is messed up too. The body language changes. Mental toughness weakens. Emotional imbalance is so conspicuous. Self-preservation is obliterated, spirits impaired, the decision-making process in total disarray. You, take care of your mindset. Everything else is taken care of.

Nobody will give you the absolute best of himself, but yourself. You must invest in the absolute best of yourself to get the best versions of yourself at any given time.

Redemption

Why should I live your dream when I have mine?

Why should I love you

As much as I love myself?

Why should I pray for you when I

Also needed redemptions?

Why should I inspire you when I

Have my own challenges?

Why should I encourage you

When I have my own weaknesses?

Why should I worry about you

When I have my own tribulations?

Why should I support your efforts

When I have my own ambitions?

Why should I fight your battles

When I have my own predicaments?

Why should I sacrifice for your triumphs

When I have my own disappointments?

Why should I laugh with you

When I am lost and afraid?

A man who lacks foresightedness is not just a failure to himself alone. A man who lacks self-discipline is not just a failure to himself alone. He is also a burden to everyone. around him.

You have to love people. You have to care about the people around you. You have to love them with tenderheartedness. They're the only family you have.

Everyone who passes through our journeys in our lifetimes are our friends. They are family. They should be treated with love. They should be treated with care. They should be treated with civility. They should be treated with benignancy.

When you are good, you're good. When you are bad, there is always room for changes. There is always more room for improvements. There is always more room for upgrading.

It's not what they think about you that matters as much as what you think about yourself. You are who you are; they are what they are. Love yourself. Take care of who you are. Take care what you represent.

Life is more delightful when you are happy. Life is more eventful when you have goals, when you have aspirations. Life is even more exciting when you have love, when you have success, when you have self-contentment.

A Day at a Time

A day at a time,

A day at a time,

A day at a time.

Take a day at a time,

Take a day at a time.

A day at a time.

A day at a time

Till you find your paths,

Till you find your solutions.

Just take a day at a time

Till the cloud dissipates.

Just take a day at a time

Till the pandemics disappear.

Just take a day at a time

Till the coronavirus goes away.

Just take a day at a time

Till you find your victories.

Just take a day at a time

Till you get to your destinations.

It takes more than simplicity to handle distinctiveness. It takes more than ordinariness to appreciate magnificence. If you don't have a clue, if you don't have the guts, if you don't have the grits, if you don't have any gumption, if you don't have any intelligence, if you don't have any audacity, if you don't have any perspicacity, you may never know how to handle exceptionalism.

A Pure Heart

Can I ever find

A pure heart,

A beautiful mind

With no blemish,

A unique mind

With no bias

Or pretense?

Can I ever find

A pure heart,

A gentle mind

With no hatred

Or discrimination?

A heart so pure,

A mind so beautiful

They embrace imperfections

Without prejudice?

Can I ever find a pure heart?

Can I ever find a beautiful mind?

Can I ever find a pure heart,

A beautiful mind

With no hatred?

A great mind

With no malice?

A unique mind

With no envy?

Can I ever find a pure heart?

Can I ever find a purified mind?

Can I ever find a pure heart,

A beautiful mind

With no blemish?

A unique mind

With no bias?

A great mind

With no prejudice?

Can I ever find

A pure heart,

A gentle mind

With no hatred?

A compassionate mind

With no discrimination?

Patience always wins the race. When things don't go right, be patient. Things will change. When life is difficult, be patient; life will change. When challenges are overwhelming, be patient. Problems will be solved. When life is unbearable, be patient. Don't kill yourself.

Life is about appreciation. Life is about celebrations. You appreciate what you have when you have it. You celebrate what you have while you have it. You believe in what you have just as you have it. Appreciate your life. Celebrate your life now that you have it.

Time Doesn't Wait

Time, like a clock,

Doesn't wait for anybody.

Time, like a clock,

Doesn't wait for anyone.

Time, like a clock,

Keeps ticking.

It keeps ticking

For success or for failure.

It keeps ticking

Irrespective of wisdom or ignorance.

It keeps ticking

Irrespective of victories or tragedies.

It keeps ticking

Irrespective of triumphs or despondencies.

Time, like a clock,

Never stops ticking.

Time, like a clock,

Never stops running.

Time, like a clock,

It keeps ticking.

It doesn't wait for anybody.

Your time, like a time clock,

Waits for no man.

A Champion

You are a champion.

A champion raises champions.

You are a leader.

A leader makes other leaders.

You are a champion.

A champion raises hope.

You are a leader.

A leader makes a difference.

Raise champions in your homes.

Make leaders at your jobs.

Raise champions in your churches.

Make leaders in your communities.

Raise champions in every setting of life.

You are a champion.

A champion raises champions.

You are a leader.

A leader makes leaders.

You are a champion.

A champion raises hope.

You are a leader.

A leader makes a difference.

Life without Dreams

Life without structures couldn't stand.

Life without dreams couldn't actualize.

Life without goals couldn't prosper.

Life without vision couldn't succeed.

Life without process couldn't function.

Life without God couldn't be superlative.

Life without structures couldn't stand.

Life without dreams couldn't actualize.

Life without goals couldn't prosper.

Life without visions couldn't succeed.

Life without discipline couldn't function.

Life without God couldn't be superlative.

Celebrations do not eventuate at the commencement but at the finishing line, when accomplishments have been established. When battles have been won. When victories have been captured. When triumphs have been claimed. When celebrations can be captured. When celebrations can be expressed; when celebrations can be implied.

The weapons you need against the challenges of tomorrow can only be acquired through the trials of yesterday, through the tribulations of today. There is no escape if you are predetermined to be above the crowds. You also have to be receptive to the challenges of today to cultivate the greater opportunities for a better tomorrow.

A little change is a big change. A little positive change makes a big difference. A small positive change will take us from the depth of the valley to the mountaintops. A little progress is a big progress. One little progress today is the commencement to a better, more fruitful tomorrow.

My God Is Always Here

My God is always here with me,

Even when things don't go well.

He is always here with me,

Even when the wind blows.

He is always here for me,

Even when the hurricane strikes.

He is still here with me.

He is my omnipresent.

He is always here for me.

He is my omnipotent.

He resides here with me.

My God is always here with me.

My God is always here with me.

Even when things don't go well,

He is still here with me.

Even when the wind blows,

He is always here for me.

Even when the hurricane strikes,

He is still here with me.

He is my omnipresent.

He is always here for me.

He is my omnipotent.

He resides here with me.

My God is always here with me.

Magnetism

Our minds are like magnets.

Whatever they attract, they bring to fruition.

Whatever they believe in, they establish.

Whatever they conceive, they implement.

Whatever they dream, they actualize.

Positive minds attract advancement.

Optimistic minds invite success.

Brilliant minds invoke dynamism.

Humble minds establish honors.

Disciplined minds impact leadership and recognition.

Our minds are like magnets.

Whatever they attract, they bring to fruition.

Whatever they believe in, they establish.

Whatever they conceive, they implement.

Whatever they dream, they actualize.

Life is Like Magic

Life, like magic,

Comes and goes.

It's here today

Gone tomorrow.

Life, like magic,

Is spontaneous like the wind.

Once gone,

It becomes a legacy.

Life, like magic,

Right now matters most.

Today dictates the precedents

For tomorrow.

Life, like magic,

Comes and goes.

It's here now

Gone tomorrow.

Life, like magic,

Is spontaneous.

Once gone,

It becomes a legacy.

Life, like magic,

Right now matters the most.

Today always dictates

The precedents for tomorrow.

No one will do for you as much as you will do for yourself. No one will love you as much as they love themselves.

It's hard to separate enemies from friends when everybody around us pretends to be our best friends.

It's almost impossible for a man to live without a fault. Yet a man is neither weak nor imprudent. What's the purpose of a man on earth other than to bless himself and to bless others? Otherwise, a man is subhuman.

A leader must love his followers more than he loves his life. Otherwise, he is just another follower.

Bed is the best friend of a lazy man. He loves his bed more than he loves his life.

You can't purchase class with money. It's either you have it or you don't. It's not necessarily the way you dress, not the expensive car you drive, or the big house you live in. It's in the reflection of the traits and characteristics you possess, that you've built over the years. It's subconsciously and emphatically embedded in your system. It's ingrained in your blood. It's entrenched in your mentality. It's established in your attributes. It's apparent in your pronouncements. It's obvious in your mannerisms. It's evident in your thought processes. Class—it's either you have it or you don't.

Class is Uniqueness

Class is uniqueness.

Personality is distinction.

Friendship is tolerance.

Consistency is dedication.

Humanity is predictable.

Advancement is evolution.

Curiosity is enlightenment.

Ignorance is backwardness.

Hostility is evil.

Excellence is discipline.

Success is hard work.

God is supreme.

Life is happiness.

Happiness is life.

Happiness is life.

Life is happiness.

Class is uniqueness.

Personality is distinction.

Friendship is tolerance.

Consistency is dedication.

Humanity is predictable.

Advancement is evolution.

Curiosity is enlightenment.

Ignorance is backwardness.

The application of the absolute best of yourself is the true representation of the absolute best of your efforts and the true expectations of the absolute best of your performances. It is the true realization of the absolute best of your personal victories.

Procrastination kills a beautiful dream. Lack of self-discipline ends a prosperous journey. Lack of effort frustrates a promising destiny.

To be a champion, you have to walk like a champion. To be a leader, you have to have the attributes of a great leader. To be exceptional, you have to have the demeanor of a transformational leader.

Use your mind to create your own dynamism. Use your mind to create your own distinctions. Use your mind to create your own success. You owe it to yourself to be above the crowd. You owe it to yourself to be special. You owe it to yourself to be above a commonality.

Friendship is Love

Friendship is love.

Friendship is loyalty.

Friendship is tolerance.

Friendship is sacrifice.

Friendship is fairness.

Friendship is compassion.

Friendship is admirable.

Friendship is loyalty.

Friendship is tolerance.

Friendship is love.

Friendship is upliftment.

Friendship is fairness.

Friendship is compassion.

Friendship is honorable.

The beauty of our lives, the magnificence of our journeys are emblematic of our adversities. They are symbolic of our personal battles, of our misfortunes, of our struggles, of our inadequacies, of our triumphs, of our victories, of our intelligence, of our successes, of our stories. They are the reflections, the fundamentals, the prognostications, the facades that capture our peculiarities. That transform our personalities. That recalibrate our mannerisms. That reshape our demeanors. That personalize our idiosyncrasies. They are the portraits of our escapades, the mirrors, of our pasts, the transgressions of our endeavors, of our performances, of our accomplishments, of our upbringings, of our failures that never leave our minds or depart from our memories. Even with the oblivion of time, it never goes away.

Personal Edification

When things are good,

It's on your own personal edification.

But when things are bad,

It's also your responsibility to make them right.

You are the stakeholder of your existence.

You are the magician of your paradise.

You are the architect of your destiny.

You are the stakeholder of your existence.

You are the magician of your paradise.

You are the architect of your destiny.

When things are good,

It's on your own personal merits.

But when things are bad,

It's also your duty to make them good again.

You are the stakeholder of your existence.

You are the magician of your paradise.

You are the architect of your destiny.

You are the stakeholder of your existence.

You are the magician of your paradise.

You are the architect of your destiny.

A man has to be a man. A man has to be conversant with himself, with his mind. A man has to be progressive minded, transcendent in his thinking. He must nurture his mind with intelligence, with bravery, with knowledge. A man has to be cognizant of his power, recognize his prowess, believe in his uniqueness. He must see wisdom in his presence, humility in his mannerisms. A man has to be bold enough in his determination. A man has to be courageous in his actions, in his declarations, in his assertions, in his pronouncements. A man just has to be a man.

A step at a time. A step at a time. A step at a time equals many steps at a time. Take a step. Take a step. Take a step at a time. Another step at a time equates to many steps at a time toward your destinations, toward your goals, toward your victories.

Can't Be Afraid

Can't be afraid of failures.

Can't be scared of challenges.

Can't be terrified of adversities.

Can't be afraid of opportunities.

When one way is blocked,

Another one will open up.

When one road is blocked,

Another one always opens up.

There is no triumph without obstacles.

There is no advancement without challenges.

There is no success without failures.

There is no tomorrow without today.

There is no end without beginning.

There is no celebration without victories.

Can't be afraid of failures.

Can't be scared of challenges.

Can't be terrified of adversities.

Can't be afraid of opportunities.

When one way is blocked,

Another one will open up.

When one road is blocked,

Another one always opens up.

We have to appreciate what we have, even if it's not good enough. We will polish it up. We will make it better. We will make it the best ever.

A man is blessed far beyond his imagination. A man is blessed far beyond his wildest dreams, far beyond his unrealistic fantasies. A man is blessed far beyond his beautiful mindsets, far beyond his superlative intelligence. A man is blessed far beyond his powerful visions, far beyond his magnificent perceptions. A man is blessed far beyond his unparalleled intellectualism, far beyond his transcendental personality.

Lack of knowledge is a deficiency. Lack of intelligence is a curse. Lack of empathy is inhumane. Lack of compassion is an aberration to the norms, to the core values of humanity.

Motivation

Walk if you must.

When you walk,

Walk as quickly

As you must.

Run if you can.

When you run,

Run as fast

As you can.

Fly if you may.

When you fly,

Fly as high

As you may.

Take advantage

Of the moment.

Do everything

To the best of your ability.

Take advantage

Of now.

Do everything

To the best of your efforts.

Walk if you must.

When you walk,

Walk as quickly

As you must.

Run if you can.

When you run,

Run as fast

As you can.

Fly if you may.

When you fly,

Fly as high as you may.

Life is a constant battle. It never stops. Can't win it all. Can't lose it all. Some we win. Some we lose. We just have to win the most important ones to make our lives more tolerable, more enjoyable, more fun-loving.

We have to be truthful to ourselves. We have to be honest with others. We have to be more transparent to others. We have to be more sincere with ourselves. We have to be more personable with who we are. We have to be more comfortable with what we bring to the table.

Loosen up. Don't take life too seriously. Life comes. Life goes. If you fall, get up. When you rise, get others up. Life is here now and gone tomorrow.

Conversation

Just thinking.

Just thinking.

I am just thinking.

I am just thinking.

Thinking about the possibility of a better tomorrow.

To anticipate the triumphs of the battles that had never begun.

To win the wars that had never been fought.

To actualize the dreams that had never been envisioned

To find the beauty of life that had never been explored.

To realize favors from humanity that had never been anticipated.

To receive mercies from Almighty God that had never been deserved.

To create platforms for a better tomorrow that had never been conceived.

Just thinking.

Just thinking.

I am just thinking.

Just thinking aloud

About the possibility of a better tomorrow.

We don't have to tell people what to do. They know the right things to do. We just have to guide them to do the right things at the right times.

When you have dreams, when you have aspirations, when you have visions, when you have goals, you have tomorrow. You have hopes, you have continuities, you have a bright future.

Negativity is not a solution; it's a problem. A negative mind is a pessimistic mind. A cynical mind is a mind that is always engrossed in the downsides instead of the upsides.

Humanity is humanity. People are people. If given the same opportunities, if given the same level playing fields, they will all rise to the challenges.

When we set the right precedents, others will follow. Setting the right precedents is by doing extraordinary things to separate distinctions from commonality. To separate actions from procrastination. To separate intellectuality from mediocrity. To separate the intelligentsia from the ignoramuses.

Mediocrity

Mediocrity is the syndrome of inferiority.

Lack of integrity is the symptom of the weaklings.

Laziness is the assertion of the failures.

Procrastination is the pinnacle of the cowards.

When we failed where others succeeded,

When we lost where others won,

When we were reactive where others were proactive,

When we were cowards where others were valiant,

When we lost the sights of reality for sentimentality,

When failure became part of our ethos and norm,

When we refused to cultivate opportunities for a better tomorrow,

We ended up in perpetual darkness without visions, hope, or love.

Mediocrity is the symptom of inferiority.

Lack of integrity is the symptom of the weaklings.

Laziness is the assertion of the failures.

Procrastination is the pinnacle of the cowards.

Everybody is an Empire

Everybody is an empire.

Everybody is an island.

Everybody is a blessing.

Our differences make us

To be more unique.

Our diversity makes us

To be more special.

Everybody is an empire.

Everybody is an island.

Everybody is a blessing.

Everybody we meet on the journeys of life should be recipients of our blessings, recipients of our kindness, recipients of our love, of our transparency, of our hospitality, of our candor, of our affections, of our benevolence, of our sincerity, of our friendship. We are all on this journey together. We're all humans; we are all the same.

You have to feel it to believe it. You have to believe it to dream about it. You definitely have to dream of it to actuate it. Success is about feeling it, believing it, dreaming it, and actualizing it.

If anyone can change, everyone can change. It's absolutely imperative that we all change for the best. It's absolutely necessary we all change for the greater versions of ourselves.

Show me your hands. It's the only way to declare your distinctions. Show me your face. It's the only way to perform your uniqueness. Show me your mind. It's the only way to demonstrate your wisdom.

When a decision is positive, the impact goes beyond ordinariness. The aftereffect goes beyond simplicity.

Life is Beautiful

Life is beautiful when you have it.

Life is unique when you have success.

Life is awesome when you have good friends.

Life is worth living when you have a loving family.

Life is beautiful when you have it.

Life is unique when you have success.

Life is awesome when you have good friends.

Life is worth living when you have happiness.

Life is beautiful when you have it.

Life is unique when you have success.

Life is awesome when you have a loving family.

Life is worth living when you have God.

Negativism leads us nowhere but to hell. Positivism opens the gates to a magnificent paradise, to unexplored territories of greatness, to our personal happiness, to our self-contentment. To our heaven.

Feels great when you love yourself. Feels more delightful when you love others. Feels much more ecstatic, much more electrifying, when they also love you back.

When you do good, standing on the pinnacle of the highest mountain can't contain your excitement. But when you do bad, even in the crowd of nonentities, you still have to hide your face in shame.

Preeminence

A man of preeminence is not a man of ordinariness.

A man of distinction is not a man of commonalty.

A man of uniqueness is not a man of self-centeredness.

A man of self-discipline is not a man of subservience.

A man of preeminence is not a man of self-centeredness.

A man of distinction is not a man of subservience.

A man of uniqueness is not a man of commonalty.

A man of self-discipline is not a man of ordinariness.

A man of preeminence is not a man of commonality.

A man of distinction is not a man of ordinariness.

A man of uniqueness is not a man of subservience.

A man of self-discipline is not a man of self-centeredness.

A man of preeminence is not a man of failures.

A man of distinction is not a man of hopelessness.

A man of uniqueness is not a man of commonalty.

A man of self-discipline is not a man of trepidations.

Everything in life takes time to mature. From infancy to adulthood takes many strides. From ordinariness to distinction takes many preparations. From poverty to self-sustenance takes self-discipline, sacrifice, knowledge, hard work.

From ignorance to wisdom takes a lot of education, takes a lot of enlightenment, takes a lot of open-mindedness.

Can't be mad at yourself for who you are. Can't be disappointed in yourself for what you have. Can't be angry at the world for who you become. Can't blame humanity for the self-image you create. Can't be overwhelmed by the challenges you face. Can't disparage others for who they are. Be happy for who you are.

We must consistently support what's right. We have to insistently condemn what's wrong. It's the only way to build a better community. It's the only way to uphold a greater society.

If you can't make it better, please don't make it worse. Leave it the way it is for someone else to make the best ever.

Faithfulness

Destiny starts with believing in yourself.

You have to believe in your mind.

You have to faith in your direction.

You have to believe in your potential.

You have to have faith in your abilities.

You have to believe in your dreams.

You have to have faith in your aspirations.

You have to believe in your representations.

You have to have faith in your choices.

You have to believe in your presence.

Destiny starts with believing in yourself.

You have to have faith in your future.

You have to have faith in your personality.

You have to believe in humanity.

You have to have faith in God.

Life is Happiness

Life is happiness.

Happiness is life.

When happiness is life

And life is happiness,

One's life is fulfilled.

Life is happiness.

Happiness is life.

When happiness is life

And life is happiness,

One's destiny is fulfilled.

Life is happiness.

Happiness is life.

When happiness is life

And life is happiness,

One's life is celebrated.

You have to love everything around you. If you don't, make some changes. When you don't, make some reparations. You have to love everything around you. If you don't, make some adjustments. When you don't, make some improvements. Make things better. It's within the confines of your capability, of your happiness, of your self-contentment, of your peace of mind, of your personal triumphs, of your victories to always love everything you have around you.

If your God is my God, if my God is your God, we are all the same. We're all descendants of the same God. We are all humans. We are all the same. We are all children of the same God.

Hold somebody's hand. Give someone a hug. Bless a stranger with a smile. Be affectionate. Be compassionate. Be kind. Love yourself. Love others. Be consistent, be courageous, be happy.

We can't intentionally be indifferent about our today. We can't intentionally be lackadaisical about our tomorrow. We can't intentionally be ignorant about our future. We can't intentionally be insouciant about our destiny. We can't afford to be ill prepared against our future challenges. We can't afford to be unpredictable about our final destinations.

You're not obliged. to be like somebody other than yourself. You're not obliged to be like anybody else but you. You're created to be the best of yourself—different, unique, and special.

A Game Plan

Have to have a game plan.

Have to have a game plan.

Have to have a game plan.

A game plan to be better than yesterday.

A game plan to move from poverty to prosperity.

A game plan to find peace and satisfaction.

A game plan to move from sadness to jubilation.

A game plan to find knowledge and enlightenment.

A game plan to find self and pathways to comfort and stability.

Have to have a game plan.

Have to have a game plan.

Have to have a game plan.

A game plan to be better than yesterday.

A game plan to move from poverty to prosperity.

A game plan to move from failure to success.

Have to have game plans to succeed in life.

The laziest way to develop personal growth is to believe solely in prayers without knowledge. The laziest way to develop great visions is to believe solely in miracles without effort. The laziest way to develop success is to believe solely in hope without performances. The laziest way to develop progress is to believe solely in fantasy without skill sets. The laziest way to develop excellence is to believe solely in superstitions without intelligence.

No one is more special than another. No one is more superior than who you are when you consistently bring your absolute best to the table, even in the dark corridors. When you constantly bring your absolute best to the table, even in the open space, in the market square, on the global stage through your personal efforts, without trepidations, through your genuine sacrifices, without reluctance, through your excellent performances without fear.

There should be a continuous progression of ascension in all our endeavors. Where there's no effort, there is no performance. Where there is no progress, there is also no effort. Where there is no victory. there's always stagnation.

It's not just the quantity of what a man has in his hands that defines his characters. It's not just the quality of what a man has in his hands that determines his success either. Rather, it is what he does or doesn't do with it to bless himself, to bless others, and to bless. all the rest of the people around him.

Every day is a new day. Every day is a new beginning. Start your today with self-confidence. Begin your new day with your best performance, with your best efforts.

Everything in Life Matters

Everything in life matters

Everything in life is essential.

Everything in life is important.

Everything in life is significant.

Everything in life is sequential.

There is no ambiguity.

There is no coincidence.

There is no turning back.

There is no regression.

Every decision is relevant.

Every mistake is pernicious.

Every reaction is contentious.

Every victory is commendable.

Every accomplishment is a triumph.

Everything in life matters.

Everything in life is essential.

Everything in life is important.

Everything in life is significant.

Everything in life is sequential.

Ordinarily, opportunity doesn't come without personal sacrifices. Personal success doesn't ordinarily come without hard work. Not without preparations, not without resilience, not without sweat, not without self-preservation.

Don't take life for granted. Every little thing matters in life. A little misstep here, a little misstep there adds up to bigger problems.

Use your mind to create your own dynamics. Use your mindset to create the best version of yourself. It's within you to always be the best version of yourself.

Just living life is not good enough. We have to live a productive life. We have to live a life full of energy, a life full of adventures. We have to live a life full of challenges. We have to live a life full of happiness. We have to live a life full of entertainment, full of celebrations.

Where there's a lack of strong leadership, there is also a lack of positive direction. Where there's a lack of great leadership, there is also a lack of pragmatism. There is also a lack of great visions, a lack of progress, and a lack of victories.

Intelligence is the ace in the game of life. When you don't have it, you've already lost the game.

We have to choose our own pathways in life. We have to pick our own friends in life. We have to find our own associates in life. We have to find our lovers. We have to find the groups we belong to. We have to be in a circle of people who care about our progress, the people who boost our morale. We have to find the people who uplift our potential. We have to find the people who celebrate our growth, people who celebrate our happiness. When we align ourselves with the wrong crowd, with the wrong friends, with the wrong partners, with the wrong families, with the wrong colleagues, we will also be measured by their inactions, by their stagnancy, by their failures. We will also be affected by their mediocrity, their ineptitudes, and their subserviency.

An excellent mannerism is a valuable asset to have. A personal wealth to possess. An unparalleled accreditation to be proud of—priceless, worth more than silver or gold.

A Clouded-Mind

A clouded mind,

Devoid

Of sunshine.

Devoid

Of illumination.

A clouded mind,

Devoid

Of excitement.

Devoid

Of happiness.

Devoid

Of self-contentment.

A clouded mind,

Ignorant

Of uniqueness.

Unconscious of Greatness.

A clouded mind, unaware

Of magnificence,

Of triumph.

Unperturbed

By the beauty

Of exquisiteness.

A clouded mind

Fails to understand the travesty

Of hatred.

Fails to understand

The negative impact

Of animosity.

Fails to accept the destruction

Of animosity.

Fails to recognize

The devastation

Of self-condemnation.

Hell or paradise is on our minds, in our thinking, in our heads, in our perceptions, in our everyday activities. In our efforts, in our performances, subject to our failures, subject to our successes, subject to our struggles, subject to our triumphs, subject to our tentativeness, subject to our proactiveness, to our misbehaviors, to our idiosyncrasies. Subject to our disappointments, to our accomplishments, to our ignorance, to our wisdom, to our weakness. Subject to our strengths, to our inadequacies, our frustrations, our comfort levels.

Since a man was beautifully made in God's image, his mind was embedded with humankind's core values, with human dynamics, with dignity, with foresight, with great insightfulness, with brilliant minds, with awesome integrity, and with great vision. A man should always represent the best in God. A man should always represent the best in humanity since a man was perfectly made in God's image.

It's a herculean task to impact a foolish mind with knowledge as his mind is already made up, preoccupied with his own misconceptions, misled by his own ignorance, blindfolded by his imbecility. And misguided by his reluctance to change.

There is no quick fix without repercussions. There is no miracle without effort. There is no self-accomplishment without performance. There is no success without sacrifice. There is no progress without performance. To appreciate heaven, you must have gone through hell innumerable times.

Mind is the Ultimate

Humanity is dynamic.

Mind is the ultimate.

Compassion is a blessing.

Life is everlasting.

Culture is formidable.

Heart is forgiving.

Language is powerful.

Pronouncement is an assertion.

Mannerism is contagious.

Comradeship is excitement.

Personality is an impression.

Society is people.

Friendship is honesty.

Respect is honor.

Family is wealth.

Love is emotion.

Tradition is refinable.

Unity is strength.

Sentiment is attention.

Hatred is foolishness.

Resiliency is courage.

Compliment is upliftment.

Division is a calamity.

It's not just the beginning that defines the results. It's not just the beginning that justifies the results. Rather, every other intangible that comes along the way to make our journeys more worthwhile, more fun, and more enjoyable.

Life is about self-interest. Life is all about accomplishing personal goals. Nothing else really matters insofar as we fulfill those obligations to effectuate our individual goals. We have done very well for ourselves.

I am an optimist. I am ready to dance without music. I am ready to fly without wings. I am ready to swim across the lagoon without thinking. I am ready to drive through the thick forest without a compass. I am ready to lay down my precious life for my beliefs. I am ready to lay down my precious life for my convictions. I am ready to lay down my precious life for my love. I am ready to lay down my precious life for my affections. I am ready to lay down my precious life for others without hesitation.

I am an optimist with an appetite for progressivism. I am an optimist with an appetite for civility. I am an optimist with an appetite for benevolence. I am an optimist with a hunger for friendship. I am an optimist with a hunger for love, with aspiration for caring without reservations, without shame. I am an optimist. I always wished people well when I shouldn't have. I aways lifted people up who I shouldn't have. I lived and dined with my enemies who pretended to be my best friends without fear, without apprehension, without trepidation. I am an optimist. I would speak my mind. when I shouldn't. I would cry when I got emotional. I would laugh so loudly when I was excited, even when the joke wasn't funny. Without apologies, I am an optimist. I would celebrate other people's successes without resentment. I would celebrate other people's victories without shame. I would celebrate other people's happiness without prejudice, without malice. I am just an optimist, and I love humanity.

Mind, Know Thyself

Mind, know thyself.

Know thy greatness.

Know thy power.

Know thy importance.

Tell the world

How mighty thou are.

Show the world

Thy brilliance.

Show the world

thy ingenuity.

Mind, illuminate thy thoughts.

Let the world know

How passionate thou are.

Mind, display thy intelligence.

Let the people know

How beautiful thou are.

Mind, show thy compassion.

Let the world know

How tolerant thou are.

Mind, know thyself.

Mind, recognize thyself.

How mighty thou are.

You shouldn't have just one best friend. You should have multiple best friends. Everyone who crosses your path, everyone who works through your pathway should also be in the position of being your best friend.

If you open your mind, you can see how beautiful. you are far beyond the physical realm. It has everything to do with your great personality through the application of your awesome mannerism, the expressions of your great attributes, and the exposure of your emulative uprightness.

It's inhumane to think you're better than others simply because of your complexion, simply because of your color, not necessarily because. of your self-representation. Nor because of the demonstration of your integrity or because of the applications of your intellect.

Self-confidence is like Viagra. It's the ultimate energy stimulant. It pumps up self-esteem beyond the realm of understanding. Self-confidence boosts courage. It boosts tenacity and optimism beyond simplicity. Self-confidence give us inexplicable excitement that energizes us beyond expectations, above ordinariness, beyond personal obligations. It gives us boldness and the audacity to stand above the crowd.

Self-confidence is the difference between winners and the losers. The difference between the timid and the courageous. The difference between the successful and the unsuccessful. The difference between the valiant and the cowardly. The difference between the champions and the mediocre.

When we are self-confident, we also have momentum. We have drive. And we have the desire to overcome the ambiguities, to overcome the trepidations, adversities, challenges, trials, and tribulations in our lives.

Self-Pride

Mine is mine.

Yours is yours.

I don't want yours;

I have mine.

I complement yours.

Will you do the

Same for me?

Yours may be better,

Maybe not.

But it's yours anyway.

Mine is mine,

Even not as good.

I will make it better.

Wish me well,

Just as I wish you.

It's a lonely journey

Without a friend

To hold my hands.

Please wish me well,

Just as I wish you well

So that you have my friendship

And my loyalty forever.

You don't have to be the best at everything you do. You just have to be the best in everything you do best.

Authenticity, integrity, and honesty are the true core values of humanity. If you have them, you're already in heaven. In a paradise of rarities, in a class of uncommonalities, devoid of superficiality, pretentiousness, deceptiveness, and misrepresentations.

It's really hard to find yourself when you don't really know yourself. It's harder to find happiness, harder to find self-fulfillment when you don't have any clue about who you are or any idea about where you are going.

We can't really be overwhelmed by our present conditions when we have tomorrow. We can't really be aggrieved about our misfortunes when we have positive tendencies. We can't really be discouraged by our adversities when we have inherent opportunities to change our situations from bad to good, from good to great, from great to excellence.

Selfishness is evil. Hatred is despicable. Hostility is counterproductive. Wickedness is deplorable. Jealousy is detrimental to self-growth. When we concentrate on the negative aspects of our strengths, the results are desolation, melancholy, and despondency. When we have bitterness and vengeance in our hearts, the aftereffects are the deprivation of spiritual maturity, insightfulness, and progressivism.

Tenaciousness

Raised my voice,

Called his name

With the intensity

Of a downtrodden.

Feared my voice

Not loud enough

To be heard.

My deeds

Not good enough.

My needs

Not as important.

My efforts

Not recognized.

Destitute with little,

Deprived from the beginning of

Opportunities to be greater

Than my dreams

To be greater

Than my aspirations

To be exceptional

Than my ambitions.

I cried.

I called his name.

Not sure

He heard me.

I called again

With pain

In my voice,

Anguish

In my soul.

Called louder.

Again and again,

Louder I called.

And I cried.

And I called again.

Nobody heard my voice

Or cared about my pains.

Nobody heard my voice

Or cared about my happiness,

Or cared about my success.

All I ever wanted was love,

Yet it I couldn't find.

It takes conscientiousness to overcome the spirits of obsession with wrongness. It takes strong willpower to overcome self-deceit and bad habits. The more wrongness we entertain in our lives, the more prevalent are failures, misfortunes, and retrogressions in our existence.

It takes clear visions, it takes persistence, it takes self-discipline; it takes more than focus to be right more often than wrong.

Victory

Victory,

I know thy name.

I know thy beauty.

I know thy pride.

I know thy joy.

I know thy happiness.

I know thy excitement.

Success,

I know thy challenges.

I know thy intricacy.

I know thy journey.

I know thy expectations.

I know thy consequences.

I know thy fulfillments.

To be victorious

Comes with trials.

To be successful

Comes with hard work.

To be exceptional

Comes with distinctions.

To be triumphant

Comes with adversities.

Victory,

I know

I have to be submissive

To thy stipulations.

Have to be obedient

To thy guidance.

Have to be receptive

To thy disciplines.

Success,

I know thy compass.

I know thy directions.

I know thy ways.

I know thy practices.

I know thy commandments.

I know thy dictations.

Victory,

I know

I have to obey

Thy callings.

Have to answer

To thy demands.

Have to celebrate

Thy success.

Have to be worthy

Of thy honors.

Repetition always brings true authenticity to perfection. It always brings true perfection to a process, to a performance, to a task, to a function. Repetition always brings the true authenticity to a behavior, a mannerism, a tradition, a culture.

Consistency through repetition always brings out the true nature of personal enthusiasm. It always brings out the true natures of our characters and the true nature of our self-disciplines. It always brings out the true natures of our commitments. Consistency through repetitions always brings the true natures of our pride and honors to perfection.

You must have a lot in common with your partner. Otherwise, your life would be a living hell, almost intolerable.

In the world of craziness, you must have audacity. You have the respect; you have the prestige. You have to have a sound mind to triumph against all odds. You must have self-discipline, courage, wisdom, and persistence to sail against adversities, misadventures, and misfortunes.

One minute you are on; the next second, you are off. One second you are up; the next minute, you are down. Can't run away from yourself. Can't shy away from realities. Can't misplace your responsibilities. Can't deny personal commitments. Can't misrepresent your beliefs. Can't ignore your mortality. Can't be intimidated by challenges to greatness, to honesty, to excellency.

Melancholy

Dazed—

Out of reality,

Out of cognizance,

Out of expectations.

Out of hope

For today

To be a little better,

Not as gloomy

As yesterday.

Not as hopeless

As tomorrow.

Oblivious

Of sunshine,

Of love.

Oblivious

Of compassion,

Of benevolence,

Of hospitality.

Unconscious

Of tenderness,

Of goodwill.

Unconscious

Of affection,

Of friendship,

Of care.

Today

Faded away

Just like

Yesterday.

Failures,

Frustrations, melancholy,

Despondency,

Sadness

In the air.

Just like yesterday.

Every day seems the same.

Just like yesterday.

Does anybody care?

Will someone care

Just a little

To give a hand

Just a little,

To love

Just a little,

To empathize

Just a little,

To have considerations,

To have feelings

Just a little?

Is that too much to ask.

Life is a recycle. What goes around always come back around. The way we treat people around us is the same way. They also turn to us what we put in to their lives. What we gave to them we will eventually get back from them.

Our lifestyles are the reflections of who we are. The reflections of our mindsets. They are the testaments of our mannerisms. The testaments of our beliefs. They are the manifestations of our attributes, of our personalities. They are the measurements of our idiosyncrasies. The aggregates of our success.

Excellent upbringing is everything in life. Great upbringing is a precursor to an outstanding commencement. A catalyst to a beautiful lifestyle. An impetus to a magnificent livelihood, to electrifying attributes, to enviable mannerisms, to admirable personal accomplishments.

You never miss anything. You never have. Nor experience something you have never encountered. Yet. You are not ignorant or lack intelligence.

My Personality

Me is me.

You are you.

You is you.

Me is me.

Personalities differ.

Me is sunshine.

You are darkness.

You are evil.

Me is righteousness.

Personalities differ.

You are sadness.

Me is happiness.

Personalities differ.

You are you.

Me is Me

I can't be you;

You can't be me.

Don't want to be you.

You don't want to be me.

Personalities differ.

Me is love.

You are hatred.

You are wickedness.

Me is compassion.

Personalities differ.

Me is me.

You are you.

Me be me.

You be you.

Me not you.

You not me.

I can't be you.

You can't be me.

I am sunshine.

You are darkness.

You have it wrong once; you have it wrong too many times. You can't afford to have it wrong too many times on the journey of life.

It takes clear visions. It takes great mindsets. It takes self-discipline. It takes self-determination. It takes great concentration to be right more often than being wrong most of the time.

Just be nice. Be nice to yourself. Be nice to everyone. We are on this journey together. You might as well be comfortable. You might as well be nice. You might as well be personable to everyone around you.

You Are One of Us

You can't be scared of humanity.

You are one of us.

You can't be afraid of death.

It comes when it comes.

You can't be tired of living.

It's the only reason you are here.

Life is sweet, but doesn't last forever.

Enjoy it now, while you're here.

Life is sweet, but doesn't last forever.

Enjoy it now that you're here.

You can't be scared of humanity.

You are one of us.

You can't be afraid of death.

It comes when it comes.

You can't be tired of living.

It's the only reason you are here.

Use your mind exquisitely to find solutions to your challenges. Use your mind brilliantly to find solutions to your situations. Use your spirits intelligently to empower your thinking faculty into preeminence. Control your emotions wisely to complement your individualism and bring it into prominence. Control your emotions imperturbably to complement your distinctions and bring into supremacy. We are all equally endowed with beautiful minds. We are all blessed with great mindsets. Our minds are the catalysts to our greatness. Our mindsets are the precursors to our excellence.

A negative mind is counterproductive to a beautiful destiny. A brilliant mind is a game changer to mediocre expectations. A mind positively utilized produces ascendancy, ingenuity, happiness, triumphs.

The applications or choices of a self-limiting mindset syndrome are self-prescribed. They are self-destructive belief that discourages the audacity to be greater than our destinies. They are a deplorable phenomenon that diminishes the boldness to be greater than our dreams. The more we elevate our minds to higher expectations, the more we surprise ourselves with accomplishments of higher magnitudes. The more we elevate our minds to higher goals, the more we surprise ourselves with greater heights of uncommon favors.

I have to outsmart myself, my mind, my ambitions, my perspectives, my intellect in order to be greater than my expectations. I have to outplay my hands, my intelligence, my tendencies, my perceptions, my intuitions in order to stand above my shoulders. I have to stand up to my ego, my pride, my narcissism, my arrogance, my prejudices in order to influence my mind to dominance. I have to humble myself to criticisms, self-discipline, self-sacrifices, self-righteousness, civilities in order to overshadow my appetite to be self-destructive.

Humility

Time flies.

Age increases.

People change.

Maturity abounds.

Wisdom multiplies.

Language improves.

Pronouncement becomes gentle.

Expressions become rich and subtle.

Understanding purified and refined.

Hair color turns to silver and gold.

Humility more commonplace.

Physicality fragile and vulnerable.

Heart grows bigger and larger

With love, kindness, and compassion.

A lazy man can't make heaven. He's already expanded his paradise on his bed, with his arms folded, waiting helplessly for God. Waiting indefinitely for a miracle from above.

If you haven't gone through hell, you will never appreciate heaven. If you haven't gone through numerous failures, you will never appreciate success. If you haven't gone through disappointments in life, you will never appreciate success.

Your life is your life. It belongs only to you. Your life is your life. It's in your hands. Your life is your life. It's in your total control. Without it, nothing else matters. Take care of yourself. Take care of your life. That's all you have.

Mind, Know Thyself

Mind, know thyself.

Know thy greatness,

Know thy power,

Know thy influence,

Know thy beauty.

Mind, tell the world

How mighty thou art,

How magnificent thou art,

How progressive thou art.

Mind, show thy world

Thy brilliance,

Thy ingenuity,

Thy compassion.

Mind, know thyself,

Know thy greatness.

Mind, sing thy praises,

How powerful thou art,

How special thou art,

How magnificent thou art.

Mind, know thyself.

Show thy world

How great thou art,

How marvelous thou art,

How mighty thou art,

How considerate thou art.

Mind, do know thyself.

A man doesn't define a situation. A situation defines a man. Put a man in a peculiar situation, you will know exactly who he is. You will definitely know what he represents.

Our lives are like books of stories. The more exciting stories we have to tell about our personal journeys, about our misadventures, the more great stories we have to tell about our challenges, our triumphs, our failures, our victories. The more magnificent journeys we've traveled, the more great people we've met, and the more eventful lives we've lived.

Complacency is an enemy of progress. The more we lie around doing nothing, the less things get done, and the less progress we make.

Not an ounce of generosity is too irrelevant to be unidentifiable. Not an ounce of hospitality is too irrelevant to be left unappreciated. When people bless us with little, we should always embrace it with love, with kindness, with gratitude.

Decency is a template, a subset of humanity. When we lack decency, we lack etiquette. When we lack decorum, we are invariably subhuman. We are invariably infrahuman.

Authenticity

Life is not superficial.

Life is real.

Life is not utopian.

Life is authentic.

Life is not a game.

Life is practical.

Life is not a fantasy.

Life is actuality.

Life is efforts.

Life is performances.

Life is wisdom.

Life is knowledge.

Life is experience.

Life is education.

Life is a process.

Life is hit and miss.

Life is trial and error.

Life is cause and effect.

Life is a chain of circumstance.

Life is what you put in and

Is what you get out.

Now you know.

The laziest way to develop personal growth is to believe solely in prayers without knowledge. It is to believe solely in miracles without skill sets.

The laziest way to develop self-confidence is to believe solely in hope without efforts. It is to believe solely in fantasies without performance. It is to believe solely in superstition without self-identity.

We don't develop intellectualism, rationalism, or greatness through only one source. Not through only one process, not through only one application, not thorough only one experience, not through only one attribute. Not through only one approach, only one race. Not through only one ethnicity. Nor do we develop intelligence, distinction, or wisdom through only one book, one religion, one tradition, one doctrine. Not through only one methodology, only one calibration, only one culture.

Brilliant minds see things in the same intelligent perspectives. Enlightened minds see things in the same intellectual mindsets. Ignorant minds also see things with the same regressive tendencies, with ill-informed, conjectural thinking, and insensitive and backward outlooks.

We have to start at the grassroots. We have to start from the basics, start from the fundamentals at the individual level. We have to start at family settings to change our courses, to improve our pathways for the betterment of our today, to upgrade our lives for the progress of our tomorrow. We must refine our cultures for the improvement of our traditions. We have to uplift our spirits for the empowerment of our mindsets. We must reverse our concentrations. We have to change our erroneous beliefs. We have to erase our selfish engagements for our legacies, for a greater tomorrow for our children, for our happiness, our pride, our nation.

Ascendancy

Positivity is the only way to ascendancy.

We have to be positive about who we are.

We have to be positive about our self-image.

We have to be positive about our self-representation.

We have to be positive about people we hang with.

Positivity is the only way to ascendancy.

We have to be positive about our self-image.

We have to be positive about who we are.

We have to be positive about people we hang with.

We have to be positive about what we represent.

Humility always wins the race. Humility will take us beyond the riversides. Humility will take us across the mighty ocean. It will take us into the land of grace. It will take us into the land of mercy.

Life is so simplistic when we embrace its true value. Life is so much fun when we are in obedience to its traditional simplistic directions. Life is very comforting when we are obligated to its cultural dictations. Life is more celebratory when we surrender our lives to its simplicity, to its comfort, to its magnificence.

Today is a new day. Today is a new beginning. Don't kill yourself over the mistakes of today. Don't hurt yourself over the failures of yesterday. Refresh, revamp, rejuvenate.

A Day at a Time

A day at a time,

A day at a time,

A day at a time.

Take a day at a time

Till you find your paths.

Take a day at a time

Till you find your solutions.

Pace … pace … pace,

Pace … pace … pace

Till you find your step.

Pace … pace … pace

Till you find your footing.

Pace … pace … pace

Till you find your comfort,

Till you find your happiness.

Just take a day at a time

Till the cloud dissipates.

Just take a day at a time

Till the pandemics disappear.

Just take a day at a time

Till coronavirus goes away.

Take a day at a time

Till you find yourself.

Nothing new aspired, nothing new gained. Everything stays the same when we are too timid to step out of our boxes. When we are too afraid to venture out of our comfort zones. When we fail to emancipate ourselves from the shackles of impotency, from the ineptitude of our lazy minds, from ignorance of our lack of sightedness. We remain stagnant. We remain unproductive. We remain backward. Nothing new is learned. Nothing new is aspired. Nothing new is gained. Everything stays the same.

Life is about people. People are about life. The more people we have in our lives, the more evolving, the more exciting, the more progressive our lives will turn out to be.

You know what to do. Just do it. Do whatever you must do to empower yourself, to emancipate your mind from the shackles of failures. To elevate your mind from the depressive situations, from ignorance, from poverty, from unhappiness, from melancholy.

Our limitations shouldn't preclude our efforts to advance. Our circumstances should not undermine our performances to greatness. Nor should our constraints diminish our distinctions to excellence.

Condescension

Don't look at me

And think

You know my name.

Don't look at me

And think

You see my heart.

Don't look at me

And think

You know my name.

Don't look at me

And think

You see my mind.

Not everyone

Who walks my way

Crosses my path.

Not everyone

Who crosses my path

Walks my way.

Not everyone

Who walks my way

Takes enough time

To know my name.

Not everyone

Who crosses my path

Is patient enough

To see my face.

Don't look at me

And think

You know my name.

Don't look at me

And think

You see my heart.

Not everyone

Who walks my way

Is kind enough

To remember my name,

Sincere enough

To look my way,

Care enough

To hold my hands,

Patient enough

To know my mind,

Kind enough

To treat me the same.

If you truly still love yourself despite all your insurmountable, overwhelming deficiencies and weaknesses, you must also love humanity despite her glaring innumerable imperfections, failures, and inadequacies. You are one of us. We are all human. We are all the same.

Love is happiness. Happiness is love. When you are loved, when you are cared for, when you are appreciated, when you are celebrated, heaven is not high enough to contain your elations, to contain your joy, your excitement, your happiness.

Show your lights to the world so that your distinctions will be felt even from the pinnacle of the highest mountains. Display your talents to society so that your uniqueness will be appreciated even from the depths of the deepest valleys. So that your peculiarities will be felt from many miles away. So that your exceptionalism will be more distinguishable. So that your life will be more remarkably impactful even in the dark corridors.

Everything in life is a memory. Just like yesterday, nothing lasts forever. We are here today, gone tomorrow. We are young today, old tomorrow. We are strong today, weak tomorrow. We are alive today, dead tomorrow. The money you selfishly hold on to becomes someone else's money. Your prestigious reputation, fancy home, expensive car, upper-class lifestyle become irrelevant. Once you are gone, your elite friends, beautiful wife, dynamic family, and exemplary pedigrees are in total oblivion. Nobody lives forever. Life is a memory, just like yesterday. Do the right thing today. Life is right now. Once it's gone, it becomes a memory. Just like yesterday.

We are all interconnected. We are all interrelated to each other. A helping hand always leads to a magical turnaround, a magnificent resuscitation that surpasses any imaginable expectations, that surpasses any sensible interpretations. A helping hand will abridge a century-long perpetual despondency, degradations, low self-esteem, and being downtrodden. A helping hand always leads to many outlets of blessing, salvation, and empowerment.

When we hold someone's hand and lead, it metamorphose to a mystical intervention, into an impact beyond ordinary. When we lead conscientiously, others follow diligently. A good leader leads positively. A biddable follower follows graciously.

Continuum

Life is a continuum.

Life is a continuity.

Life is ever progressive.

Life is ever evolving.

Life is ever everlasting.

Within her majestic undertone,

Irrespective of excuses,

Ignorance, or lack of awareness,

The continuum persists like the flow of the river.

If you get it, you get it.

If you don't, then you don't.

Life moves on.

As it was in the beginning,

So it is.

So shall it be.

Life evolves.

Life continues

With you or without you.

Life is a continuum.

It's ever evolving,

Ever progressive,

Ever everlasting.

Success and failure are opportunity costs. You can't have them both simultaneously. You must pick one or the other. It's up to you. It's your choice. It's your decision. It's your life.

You can't stop living. You can't stop running. You can't stop being open-minded. You can't stop being in search of yourself. You can't stop being inquisitive about your better self. You can't stop loving yourself.

An excellent mannerism is a valuable asset to have. It's an emblem of personal wealth to embrace, unparalleled accreditations to celebrate, a great reputation to claim, an awesome integrity to display. It is priceless, worth more than silver, more than gold.

We must choose our own pathways in life. We must pick our own friends. We must fight our own battles. We must locate our own associates. We must find our own lovers. We must prefer our own groups. We must be in the circles of the people who boost our morals. We must be in the congregations of people who uplift our potentials. People who celebrate our happiness. People who applaud our success. When we align ourselves with the wrong crowd, when we hang around the wrong friends, when we associate ourselves with the wrong partners, when we belong to the wrong families, when we prefer the wrong colleagues, when we marry the wrong spouses, we will be measurable. We will also be affected by their inactions, by their shallow-mindedness, by their stagnancy, by their failures, by their mediocrities, by their ineptitudes, by their lack of self-confidence.

A clear conscience is synonymous with heaven. When you have it, you have the ultimate satisfaction of personal triumphs, victories, self-contentment, and peace of mind.

Everything in life starts with self and ends with self. When a man fails to realize his own potential, when he fails to perceive his capability through ignorance, through ineptitude, through lack of vision, through lack of opportunity, the result is always calamity. The result is always frustration. The result is always failure.

My Color

Most people judge

A character,

A difference,

A uniqueness,

A distinction

Way ahead of their time.

Far beyond their visions,

Far away from their sights,

Far away from their perceptions,

Far beyond their understanding.

They never take the time

To know your name

Before they give you a name

That doesn't necessarily

Belong to your face.

They already condemned you

Outright before they heard your voice.

They already branded you a loser

Before they even saw your face.

They are all the same.

That's what they said.

They already killed you

Premeditatively,

Before they see your face,

Before they know your name.

Yet, they feel no remorse.

Yet, they feel no pain.

Yet, they hated to be judged.

"Hypocrisy," I shouted.

We are all the same.

We're all humans.

We are all the same.

I feel your pain.

Do you feel my mine too?

Your hypocrisy is abnormal.

You're not better than I,

Not because of your complexion.

You are not greater than I

because of your race.

Not because of your tribe,

Ethnicities, or genders.

Nor because of your status.

Nor because of your wealth.

I am still you.

You are still me.

If we trade places,

I say very loudly,

You are me,

And I am you.

We are all the same.

Life is daily. Every day is relevant. Today is as important as yesterday, just as yesterday was as important as tomorrow. Your deeds today will justify your activities or your reactions from yesterday. Just like your deeds from yesterday have justified your conditions or your positions today. Positive attitudes will always triumph over negative reactions, whether today, yesterday, or tomorrow.

Life is a delicacy with a delicate measure that merits positive outcomes. Every move is subjective. Every approach is relevant. Every idiosyncrasy is measured by decisions we make and by the actions undertaken.

Life is a delicacy. The inedible fruits we can't have enough of, yet with a taste of bitterness we can't ignore, and we can't get rid of.

Hostility downgrades positive energy. When we are always close-minded, antagonistic to positive changes through our rigidity to openness, the opportunity for positive energy is farfetched. Prosperity, success, and happiness are also far removed.

Unconsciousness

Everyone is ignorant

Standing all alone.

Everyone is insufficient

By being all alone.

Everyone is limited

Standing all alone.

Everyone is incomplete

By being all alone.

Standing with others

Makes us more resolute.

Standing with others

Makes us stronger.

Standing with our people

Makes us more resourceful.

Standing with others

Makes us more powerful.

Standing with our people

Makes us more complete.

Everyone is ignorant

By standing all alone.

Standing alone,

Standing alone,

Just by standing

All alone by himself.

No one should be more worthy to you than you. After your demise, life still goes on, still celebrated, still enjoyed. Enjoy your life now, while you can. You owe it to yourself to live the best your life on earth (heaven) while you're still here.

We all have to earn our blessings. When we do good, our rewards are assured. When we do bad, the retributions are even more reassuring.

It's not just what you have in your hands that determines the result. It's always how magnificently you play what you have that will ultimately actuate your result. You have to play it big to make it big. You have to take a chance to make a bigger splash.

A sacrifice always brings its own rewards. When we bless others, the reward is enormous. When we bless them at our expense, the reward is even more monumental.

Foolishness

In his ignorance,

A coward

Celebrates himself,

In his imbecility,

A coward

Overrides the joy

Of his brightness.

In his arrogance,

The crazy

Celebrates

His madness.

In the market squares with the Crown of

Stupidity on the head

Of his majesty,

His ignorance

So pervasive.

The smell of his imbecility,

So explosive in the open space.

Yet the fool

Celebrates his mediocrity

With impunity,

With arrogance,

With buoyancy.

The elitists too muted

To raise a hand.

The wise too senile

To remember their voices.

The intellectuals too timid,

Too blind sided

To speak their minds.

So a coward rules

With impunity.

The mediocre

Become the kings.

The dimwits

Become the intellectuals,

Wisdoms In exile,

In oblivion perpetually.

The bastards,

The barbarians,

The outcasts,

Become

Our lords.

The application of the absolute best of yourself is the remedy for your misfortunes. It is the solution to your sadness, your frustrations, your low self-esteem.

The law of concentration states that whatever we dwell on, believe in, dream of, pronounce on, make a declaration on always comes to reality.

You have to learn through yourself to find yourself, to know yourself, to really know who you truly are.

Wisdom doesn't come without pain, without anguish, without trials. Not without challenges or tribulations.

When you positively impact a life, you've blessed more than a village. When you destroy another life, you've damaged more than a society.

Subjugation

Money is gold.

Money is God.

Money is power.

Money is gold.

Money is life.

Life is money.

Money is everything.

When you don't have it,

You ain't got anything else.

When you don't have it,

You ain't got nothing.

You don't have God.

You don't have any support.

You don't have God.

If you don't have any money,

You don't have any love.

You don't have anything else.

You don't have gold.

You don't have silver.

You don't have copper.

You don't have joy.

You don't have happiness

When you ain't got money.

You ain't got anything else

When you ain't got money.

You don't have anyone on your side.

You don't have life.

You don't have pride.

You don't have friends.

You don't have lovers.

You don't have families.

You don't have recognition.

You don't have a name.

Everyone in our circle brings something different, brings something extraordinary, brings something distinctive, something peculiar, something unique, something resourceful to the table. Something more exciting, more challenging, more electrifying. Something different from our own repertoire. Different from our own experiences, our own. preoccupations. We can't be afraid of our own. We can't run away from ourselves. We can't run away from our own people. We are all the same but with a different fragrance of colorization, of distinctiveness emanating from our individual personalities, from our own dispositions.

Maturity is not defined by age alone. It also encompasses the applications of intelligence. It also encompasses the expression. of wisdom. It also encompasses the implication of etiquette, the considerations of open-mindedness, the declarations of integrity that underscore enviable attributes, that promotes progressive mannerisms, that honors magnificent personalities.

Consistency creates the same mindsets. Consistency creates the same discipline. Consistency creates the same methodologies, applications, and processes. Reliability creates the same calibrations. Reliability creates the same approaches. Reliability creates the same integrity, the same sacrifices, the same effectiveness, the same results.

We can only go as far as we can see. We can only see as far as we can go. We can only succeed as far as our knowledge. We can only be comfortable as far as our intelligence. We can only be happy as far as our efforts, as far as our performances, as far as our accomplishments.

Iyawo Mi

Can you hear me?

Can you hear me?

Can you hear me?

Iyawo mi,

Can you hear me?

When I call your name,

Baby mi,

Can you hear me?

When I say I care,

Can you hear me?

When I say you're mine,

Baby mi, can you hear me?

Iyawo mi, can you hear me?

Can you really hear me

Whenever I call your name?

Can you really hear me

Whenever I say you're mine?

Can you hear me?

Can you really hear me?

Whenever I say I care,

Can you feel me?

Baby mi, can you feel me

Whenever I touch your face?

Can you feel me

Whenever I kiss your lips?

Can you feel me

Whenever I hold your hands?

Whenever I call your name?

Whenever I touch your heart?

Iyawo mi, can you hear me?

Ife mi, can you feel me?

Iyawo mi, can you really hear me

Whenever I sing your songs?

Baby mi, can you really feel me

Whenever I play your games?

Iyawo mi, can you still love me

Whenever you feel my pains?

Whenever I say you're mine?

Baby mi, can you hear me,

Iyawo mi, can you feel me

Every time I say you're mine?

Everyone needs someone to hold his hands at one time or another. In life, everyone needs someone to pump him up beyond mediocrity. We all need someone. to lift our souls beyond simplicity. Everybody needs someone to elevate his mindset beyond failures, to lift his emotions beyond despondency. We all need someone who will always watch our backs, who will always watch our blind spots, even when no one else is paying attention.

If you're struggling to get to a destination, don't stop. Don't quit. Don't get discouraged. Be focused. Be disciplined. You will get there eventually. The longer it takes, the more fun, the more adventures, the more experiences, the more versatility. The more wisdom you also earn along. the way. And the more friends you also make on your journeys.

An intellectually gifted transformational or transcendental leader is not weary of head-on collisions, not afraid of head-on collisions against adversities, against absurdities, against animosity. Not concerned about head-on-collisions against immorality, against confrontations, against ignorance, against irregularities. Not perturbed about head-on-collisions against inhumane mannerisms, criticism, and misconceptions against ill-founded beliefs. Against misleading doctrines and misinformed assertions, to make the right impressions to change the status quo. He is not scared to right the wrong cultures, to refine the old, primitive, common practices. He is not too timid to end unethical traditions through deliverance of positive changes, through personal sacrifices, through progressive advancements for his people.

Light is the difference between darkness and. sunshine. When it refuses to shine, when it refuses to sparkle, when it refuses to illuminate, to brighten; darkness stays the same—rigid, impenetrable, unapproachable, inaccessible, ungovernable, unfathomable. Just like ignorance over knowledge. Just like sadness over happiness. Just like a cloud over sunshine.

It takes more than ordinary commitments to make bigger splashes. It takes more than inconsistent efforts to make impactful changes. It takes more than mediocre performances to make remarkable impressions. It takes more than. lackluster efforts to revise generational failures. It takes more than wrong declarations to resuscitate the old, dilapidating dynasties. It takes more than guts to stand alone amid a bigger crowd.

Obscurity

If only I know where I am going,

I can always find my way.

If only I know where I am going,

I can plan my journeys.

If only I know where I am going,

I can always plan my life.

I can always find my destinations.

I will know when to run

Or when to fly.

I will know when to walk

Or when to crawl.

I will know who to hang with

Or who to run away from.

I will know who my friends are

Or who pretends to be my lovers.

I will know where to be

And when to be there.

If only I know where I am going,

I can always find my pathways.

If only I know where I am going,

I can always find my name.

If only I know where I am going,

I can always follow my dreams.

I can always plan my journeys.

I can always find my joy.

I can always find my passion.

I can always find my love.

Only if I know where I am going,

I will have found my happiness.

To be ordinary in life takes less effort, takes less attention, takes less commitments. To be a pedestrian in life takes less preparation, less endeavors, less performances. It takes less engagements, less activities, less proactiveness, less skill sets. It takes less passion, less obligations, less discipline, less ambition, less sacrifices, less concentration to be a disappointment. To be a failure in life.

It takes more than hard work to be extraordinary. It takes more than impeccability to be admirable. It takes more than resiliency to be special. It takes more than self-righteousness to be accomplished. It takes more than uprightness to be great. It takes more than miracles to be a success in life.

Uniqueness is not a matter of ordinariness. Distinction is not a matter of simplicity. Success is not a subject of timidity. They all come with great expectations of tenacity. With great expectations of resiliency. With great expectations of persistence. With great expectations of perseverance, self-discipline, consistency, self-preservation, and great expectations of self-orientation.

Distinctions don't struggle with mediocrity. It always separates itself. Sunshine is not intimidated by the ferocity of the darkness. It always infiltrates. It always penetrates. It always dominates.

It's not only what goes through a man's mind that defines his true character but what he actually does or doesn't do with it to differentiate himself from the crowd of ignorance. From the congregations of nonentity. From the convergence of mediocrity. That is what sets him apart.

Failure

Failure,

Like a poison,

Eats you up

In and out,

Day in,

Night out.

Destroys all the

Fabrics of

Hope and happiness.

Failure,

Like a bad attitude,

Destroys and

Disrupts

Momentums,

Creates

Self-doubts,

Ambiguities,

And self-degradations.

Failure,

Like a darkness,

Keeps your brightness

Perpetually hidden

In obscurity,

Ignorant

Of time,

Ignorant

Of opportunity,

Ignorant

Of joy,

Of success,

Of self-contentment,

Of peace of mind.

Failure,

Like a menace

Threatening the

Brightness,

Sunshine,

Moonlight,

Illumination,

The tranquility

Of your existence.

Failure,

Like a predator,

Menacing,

Advancing,

Threatening,

Shakaring

The life,

The progress,

The civilization,

The advancement

Of humanity.

Money is not everything. Money is not the root of all evil as it is being misrepresented, misproclaimed, misconstrued. The evil among exists in people's minds. It is their insatiable wants, their uncontrollable desires, their outrageous demands at all costs. Money is just an instrument, a tool of progressivism. Money shouldn't be the devil. Money shouldn't be our gods. People are the devils. People are the gods. People are the players, not the money they have in their hands. Not the. money they have in their pockets. Rather, it is their arrogance, their evil-mindedness, their cold-hearted mindsets that make money become their gods, to become their goddesses, to become their devils.

Stagnancy

Everything is in the same circle.

Everything stays in the same place.

Everyone is in the same place.

Everyone stays in the same circle.

Everything stays in the same place.

Everyone stays in the same circle.

Everyone always stays in the same circle.

Everything always stays in the same place.

People hardly change their strides.

People hardly change their stances.

People hardly change their mannerisms.

People hardly change their attitudes.

People hardly change their movements.

People hardly change their thinking.

People hardly change their games.

People hardly change their minds.

No forward-going.

No progress made.

No forward-coming.

No changes assumed.

No forward-going

No evolution evoked.

No forward-coming.

No ingenuity acclaimed.

No innovations conceived.

No beauty acquired.

No magnificence celebrated.

No glory established.

No celebrations performed.

No happiness in the air.

Everyone is in the same circle.

Everything stays in the same place.

Everything is the same place.

Everyone stays in the same circle.

Everything is the same circle.

Everybody stays in the same place.

Everybody stays the same.

Everything stays the same.

And no progress made.

You are on your own. Good friends are hard to find. Best friends are harder to come across. You are your own best friend. You are your own worst enemy. When you rise, everybody rises with you. When you fall, no one is down to lift you up.

Courage, tenacity, self-confidence are the weapons of the game changers. When we refuse to give up on ourselves, when we refuse to give up on our dreams, when we refuse to give up on our lives' challenges, on our lives' expectations, we end up with victories. We end up with triumphs. We end up with celebrations. We end up with self-contentment.

Ignorance is a deficiency. When the hunger for knowledge, when the hunger for wisdom is lacking, there is always a natural tendency for our minds, our spirits, our emotions to drift toward disorder, chaos, inopportunity, heresy.

Mediocrity is a curse. Lack of intelligence is a deprivation. Lack of knowledge is a degradation, an anomaly. When we are shortchanged in the realities of life, when we are deprived of the best of our existence, when we settled for little or for nothing, life becomes more intolerable. Life becomes more indefensible with unwarranted subjugations, undeserved tribulations, and insurmountable challenges.

It takes more than simplicity, it takes more than normality to deal with extraordinary measures. If you don't have the clue, if you don't have the guts, if you don't have the grit, if you don't have the gumption, if you don't have the perceptions, if you don't have the intelligence, if you don't have the heart, if you don't have the audacity, if you don't have the perspicacity, you may never know how to handle exceptionalism.

IFeMi

IFeMi,

I really want to hold you.

I really want to hold your hand.

I really want to hold you.

I really want to care for you.

I really want to embrace you.

I really want to love you.

I really want to hold your hands.

I really want to love you.

I really want to hold your hands.

I really want to embrace you.

I really want to touch your face.

I really want to care for you.

Every time I see you,

I just want to hold you.

Every time I set my eyes on you,

I just want to touch your face.

Every time I see you,

I just want to tell you

How much I love you.

Every time I set my eyes on you,

I just want to let you know

How much I care.

Every time I set my eyes on you,

I just want you to know that

I really want to hold your hands.

I really want to talk to you.

I really want to care for you.

I really want to love you.

I really want to embrace you.

Always in my arms, Iyawo mi.

Nobody should be more worthy to you than yourself. After your demise, life still goes on. Life is still celebrated. Life is still enjoyed. Enjoy your life now, while you can. You owe it to yourself to live the best of your life on earth (heaven) while you're still here.

You can't be half good. You can't be half righteous. You can't be half bad. Uprightness, righteousness, being good are about consistency. It's about being good. It's about being righteous. It's about being upright all the time. Anything contrary to that, or in between, is heresy, a contradiction. It's a. fake. It's a fraud, unorthodox, a heterodoxy.

Life is about individualism. Life is about one's accomplishments. Life is about individual efforts and personal performances. Life is about self-motivation. The more you put in, the more you get out. The less you put, and you will be lucky if you ever get anything back in return.

A great personality always makes something so ordinary into something so distinctive. Something so simplistic into something so special. A great mind is always remodeling, always repackaging, always reinventing something so average, so commonplace into something so beautiful, so unique, so preeminent.

It's not good enough just to be human without being submissive to human core values. It's not good enough just to be human without being submissive to human traits. It's not good enough just to be human without being submissive to human worth, without being submissive to human dynamics, without being submissive to human expectations.

Iwa Lewa

When you good,

Be always good.

When you good,

Be excellently good.

When you good,

Stay always good.

Be always good.

Consistency matters.

Be always good.

Excellency matters.

Be always good.

Uniqueness matters.

When you good,

Stay always good.

A good character to have,

A better name to bear.

A great reputation to admire,

An awesome distinction to acclaim.

An enviable recognition to enjoy.

When you good,

Be always good.

Stay always good.

Be consistently good, Iwa lewa o!

It takes a leader to lead. It takes a charismatic leader to do something special. In every situation where he sees wrongs, he makes them right.

Whatever is worth doing is worth doing best. Whatever is worth doing is worth doing to the best of our abilities.

Don't hide yourself from yourself. Don't hide yourself from others. Don't deprive yourself of the best of yourself.

A man who loves himself, a man who loves his family, who loves his friends and his people, a man who loves his country and his neighbors, and who has fear of God is a well-accomplished man. A man of wealth, a man of uprightness, a man of integrity, a man of righteousness, a man of enviable character.

You can't really ignore or deny the beauty of humanity. When you have a beautiful mindset, you can't honestly condemn or reject dynamism when it's staring you right in your face.

Uniqueness is a blessing. A blessing is a distinction. A distinction is an ascendency. It's not just what you have, it's who you are. It's not just how you are, it's what you are. It's not just the symbols you create, it's the dynamism you possess. It's inscribed in your ethos, in your personality. It's displayed in your self-representations, in your pronouncements. It's apparent in your dispositions and in your discipline. It's apparent in your attitude. It's obvious in your mannerisms. It's in your aura. It's in your blood and in your preeminence. When you are unique, you are special. You are different; you are progressive. When you are distinctive, you are blessed with unparalleled qualities, with an upside that is irreplaceable, inalienable, enviable, and irreproachable.

Individualism

Find your name

So that you will answer

To your callings.

Find your name

So that you will recognize

Your journeys.

And when your name

Is called,

You can make

Your waves.

Know your name

So that you can answer

Your callings.

Know your name

So that you can recognize

Your destiny.

When your name

Is called,

You make

Your stands.

Call your name

So that they will answer

To your callings.

Call your name

So that they will know

Your stories.

When your name

Is called,

They have already

Known your destiny.

They have already

Known your destinations.

They have already known

Your face.

People around you are the most important and influential people in your life at any given time. When you invest in their lives positively, the dividend will be enormous. When you love them affectionately, the reward will be overwhelming. When you respect their opinions indiscriminately, their trust will be immeasurable. When you lead them righteously, their loyalty will be unprecedented. When you compliment them genuinely, the impression will last forever.

Distinction doesn't struggle with mediocrity. It always separates itself. Nor is sunshine intimidated by the ferociousness of the darkness. It penetrates, it dominates.

Humility is the submission of humanity to imperfection. When we are humble, irrespective of our status, we have eventually simplified the most intricate part of the complexity of humanity. It's overhyped and overexaggerated that humanity is infallible because of class, power, principality, and prestige.

De Blind Side

How come you can't see me

Even when I raise my hands?

How come you can't see me

Even when I am sitting next to you?

How come you can't hear me

Even when I raise my voice?

How come you can't hear me

Even when I sing my songs?

How come you can't love me

Even when I give you my heart?

How come you can't love me

Even when I give you my soul?

How come you can't see me

Even when I raise my hands?

How come you can't see me

Even when I am sitting next to you?

We can't really be overwhelmed about our present conditions. We can't really be aggrieved about our adversities. We can't really be discouraged about our misadventures when we have tomorrow, when we have positive tendencies, when we have inherent opportunities to change our situations from bad to good, from good to great, from great to excellent.

Selfishness is evil, hatred is despicable, hostility is counterproductive, wickedness is deplorable, and jealousy is detrimental to self-growth. When we concentrate on the negative aspects of our strengths, the result is desolation. When we have bitterness in our hearts, the aftereffect is deprivation of spiritual maturity, deprivation of insightfulness.

Kabiyesi

Eledumare,

BabaLoke,

Olodumare,

BabaMiLoke.

Iba oooooooooo Kabiyesi oooooo.

Don't play with my God.

Don't play with fire.

Don't play with my God.

Don't play with fire.

Don't play with BabaMiLoke.

Don't play with Olodumare.

I called him,

I called his name.

I called him,

I called his name.

BabaLoke,

Eledumare,

BabaLoke,

Olodumare.

I called him.

In my troubles

I called his name.

In my desperation,

I called him.

In my loneliness,

In my failures,

I called his name.

In my despondency,

I called him.

In daylight,

Late at night,

I called his name.

And he answered.

BabaMiLoke,

He always answered me.

Every time

I called his name,

He answered me.

Every time

I called his name,

He answered me.

Eledumare,

BabaLoke,

Olodumare,

Kabiyesi o.

Ignorance is darkness without rays of light. Lack of knowledge is a dead end. A clouded mind is a hell without sunshine. Life without a direction, without a purpose is a journey without a compass. An endless journey without a destination.

You don't know yourself until you find yourself. Not until you find your distinctions, not until you find your uniqueness, not until you find your strengths, not until you find your passions, not until you find your lovers, not until you find your happiness. Then you have found yourself.

My Lady

Can I feel you?

Can I touch you?

Can I feel you?

Can I touch you?

Can I feel you, my lady?

Can I touch your heart, my lady?

Can I feel your spirit, my lady?

Can I touch your soul, my lady?

Can I feel your emotions, my lady?

Even in obscurity, even in open space, in corner space of your heart, in your deepest, in your most private, in your innermost, can I have a moment? Can I just have a corner just to stay for a moment? Can I just have a spot, my lady, in your heart? Can I just hold your hands even just for a minute, my lady?

Nakedness

Life is an open space.

It has no hidden places.

Life is an open space.

It has no hidden agendas.

It has no beginning;

It has no end.

It has no happiness.

It has no bitterness.

It has no sorrow.

It has no sympathy.

It has no triumphs.

It has no failures.

Life is an open space.

It has no hidden places.

Life is an open space.

It has no hidden agendas.

It has no victories.

It has no sadness.

It has no celebrations.

It has no enemies.

It has no friends.

It has no prejudices

It has no champions;

It has no losers.

Life is an open space.

It has no hidden places.

Life is an open space.

It has no hidden agendas.

It has no biases.

It has no favors.

When you are here,

It's here with you.

When you aren't here,

It's still here without you.

It's cowardice to be quiet when we should be the loudest voices in the crowd of ignoramuses. In the congregations of the dimwits. It may change the course of a life. It may reverse the plight of a community. It may even improve the progressions of a society. It may magnificently transform the standing of a nation when we instantaneously rise to always right the wrongs rather than sit idly, doing. nothing but expect miracles from the above.

Repetition always brings the true authenticity to perfection. It always brings perfection to a process, to a performance, to a. task, to a function, to a behavior, to a mannerism, to a tradition, to a culture. Consistency through. repetition always brings out the true nature of our personal enthusiasm, of our characters, of our disciplines, of our commitments, of our pride, of our honors to perfection.

The guy who stands next to you is your brother as much as your blood brother miles away. Hold his hands. Guide him. Love him as much as you love yourself. The brother next to you is more instrumental than the ones who live miles away.

Leadership is one of the most important components of human evolution. Without great leaders among us in our communities, in our societies, and in our nations, development and advancement will be seriously hindered. We need visionary leaders who inspire new waves of new ideology, new philosophies, and different perspectives on inclusiveness, relationships, priorities, commitments, and progressive dynamics that bring impactful changes to our world.

Every pathway that crosses your path brings a different dynamics into your life. Everyone who crosses your path brings something distinctive into your existence. Pay attention.

The audacity to be great, to be special, doesn't come with timidity. Doesn't come with trepidations about the unknown. Rather, it comes with boldness, with courage to find solutions to our intricate problems that are left unresolved.

Empowerment to wrong philosophical impressions, to wrong philosophical assertions through our mind's submissiveness, to the wrong ideologies, to the negative ethos, to wrong traditions are very counterproductive to our self-accreditation and very damaging to our self-consciousness to positively manage our lives, to smartly navigate our existence according to our self-prescribed beliefs, values, and norms.

Life is the ultimate, irrespective of constraints. Irrespective of limitations. Irrespective of adverse conditions. Life is the optimum. When you have it, it's the best thing you could ever have, while you have it. It's very exhilarating to have good people. around us. People who influence our moods. People who elevate our enthusiasm. People who reignite our motivations. People who refines our attributes. People who promote our happiness. People who lift our spirits to the pinnacle of exuberance every time they are around us.

There is an inherent opportunity, a natural endowment, for humanity to be greater than themselves. Greater than their deficiencies, above their incompetence, greater than their inadequacies. We are beautifully created with natural abilities, with perfectly sound minds, with self-awareness to navigate our lives, to control our situations, to dominate, our environments. We can live above our struggles. We can live beyond our predicaments. We can live above our tribulations through a progressive approach. Through spiritual empowerment, through intrinsic motivation, through mental toughness.

When you are a winner, you are a champion. When you are a champion, you are a winner. You are a success, a warrior, accomplished. Nobody can stand in the way of your accolades. Nobody can stand in the way of your triumphs. Nobody can stand in the way of your achievements irrespective of hostilities, malevolence, and aspersions.

Orisha

Obinrin is Orisha.

A woman is a goddess.

Obinrin is Orisha.

A woman is a goddess.

Obinrin is Orisha.

A woman is a deity.

When she holds your hands

With love, with passion, with loyalty,

Orisha blesses you

With wealth, with pleasures, with comforts,

With friendship, with comradeship, with affections.

When you hold her hands

With love, with loyalty, with care,

Orisha blesses you

With sunshine, with moonlight, with happiness.

When you hold her hands,

When you hold her hands

With gold, with copper, with silver,

Orisha blesses you

With satisfaction, with joy, with happiness.

Obinrin is Orisha.

A woman is a goddess.

Obinrin is Orisha.

A woman is a goddess.

Obinrin is Orisha.

A woman is a deity.

I have to fly like an eagle with tenacity of a tiger, with the ferocity of a lion. I have to push myself like an elephant, tramping on adversities with temerity, with self-pride to dominate my environment. With class to manage my life, with resilience to promote my ambitions, to assert my goals like a ferocious shark, with self-confidence to succeed, and the audacity to triumph. I have to walk like a champion with abilities to win battles. With self-preservation to proclaim victories and to celebrate success.

Individualism is the core of human evolution. It's the core of human progressivism. When individualism is positively influenced, when individuals are greatly enriched, our collective advancement, our collective civilization, will also be significantly enhanced.

Excellent decisions are essential to our success. Great personal choices are very significant to our pride. They're the primal to the evolution of our self-identity, of the progression of our happiness.

I am an optimist. I'm always looking forward to tomorrow.

If anybody can change, everybody can change. It's a must. We all change or the best.

A man has to be a man. A man has to be self-conscious of himself. A man has to be self-aware of his capabilities, cognizant of his proficiencies to succeed against all odds, irrespective of the magnitude of the challenges to succeed. Irrespective of the persistent threat of failure in every facet of our endeavors. Yet things still have to be done in the right way, within the facade of defined protocols, within the structures of the defined norms, within the confines of the defined cultures, within the constraints of the defined traditions.

Can I Be Myself?

Can I be happy with myself

Without apologies to others?

Can I smile when I want to

Without any pretentiousness?

Can I give my heart to people

Without fear of regrets?

Can I speak my mind

Without being afraid?

Can I be myself?

Can I ever be myself?

Can I be myself?

Can I ever be myself?

Can I be myself?

Can I be myself

Without someone telling me

How to be myself?

Can I ever be myself

Without someone telling me

What to say or how to think,

Without stepping on someone else's toes,

Without feeling like I did something wrong,

Without feeling sad and apologetic?

Can I ever dance my steps

Without someone else

Telling me how to dance?

Can I dance to my music

Without someone saying

Something cynical about my steps?

Can I dance to my steps

Without someone saying something crazy

About my shoes,

Without someone saying something stupid

About my styles,

Without someone saying something crazy

About my name,

Without someone saying something outrageous

About my complexion?

I am the only one

Who knows where

My heaven is.

I am the only one

Who knows where

My hell is hidden too.

I am the only one

Who can find my journeys.

I am the only one

Who can find my pathways.

I am the only one

Who knows my heart.

I am the only one

Who knows my mind.

I am the only one

Who knows the truth.

I am the only one

Who knows the lies.

I am the only one

Who can find my paradise.

Since a man was beautifully made, his mind was greatly influenced by and nurtured with human values and embedded with norms, traits, honors, cultures, distinctions, and with personal integrity. A man should be able to be cognizant of the best of himself. A man should appreciate his attributes. He should understand his uniqueness and control his demeanor. A man should be able to represent the absolute best of himself. He should be able to promote the best in humanity without reservations, without reluctance, without arbitrariness, without condescension, without subjugation. A man should be able to have the boldness to represent the best of himself without trepidation, without fear, without condemnation.

A true leader always leads conscientiously with a caring hand and an empathetic heart, finding solutions to difficult problems, righting the wrongs, creating opportunities for others, raising the champions and empowering the great leaders of tomorrow while others talk, dream, fantasize, overthink, and do nothing.

Loneliness

The spark of my life just left.

The spark of my love just left.

The spark of my life just disappeared.

The spark of my love just left the room,

Left me all alone.

Yet I don't want the spark to leave.

Yet I don't want the spark to go away.

Yet I don't want the spark to disappear.

Yet I don't want the spark to leave me.

Yet I don't want the spark to leave the room.

Don't want the passion of intimacy just to vanish.

Don't want the spark to just disappear into oblivion.

Yet reluctant to accept the consequences of my failures,

Failed to accept the responsibility for my loneliness,

Of my ineptitude, of my melancholy, of my frustrations,

Of my lackadaisicalness.

Of my despondency.

Reluctant to hold on to the courage of my pride.

Afraid to lay acclaim to my brilliant mind.

Too timid to stand rigidly to my own personal convictions.

Too reluctant to hold my hands firmly on to

The subserviency of my heart to love.

Refused to be submissive to the subjugation of my soul.

Scared to be addicted to the soft tenderness of your touches,

Of your kisses,

Of your

Sweetness.

The love of my life just left the room.

The room looks so empty,

So quiet, so dilapidated,

So cloudier than yesterday.

So lifeless than the stagnant water.

The spark of my life just

Disappeared.

The light of the room left,

And the room turned into obscurity.

Yet, I don't know what to do.

Yet, I don't know where to go.

Yet, I don't have answers to my frustrations.

Yet, I don't have no acclaim to my pride.

Yet, I don't have any shelter to seek.

Yet, I don't have any room to sleep.

Yet, I don't have anywhere to turn.

When you pay close attention to the people around you, you can easily point out those who truly care about you against those who are just pretending to tolerate your existence.

Every day should be the best day of your life. Every minute should be the happiest moment of your existence. Every year should be the greatest year of your ascendancy. Otherwise, you're doing something wrong.

Nobody can stop you from you being you but you. Nobody can stop you from being yourself but you. Nobody can stop your progressions in life but your mannerisms. Nobody can stop your success but your character. Nobody can stop your happiness but your choices. Nobody can be in the way of your victories but your integrity. Everything you have or don't have is all about yourself. It's all about your personal choices. It's about the personal decisions you've made over your lifetime through your mindsets, through your personal beliefs, through practical application of your mannerisms to be who you are today.

Nothing is Ever Too Late

There is nothing too late beyond reparations.

There is nothing too late beyond changes.

There is nothing too late beyond progressions.

There is nothing too late beyond advancement.

There is nothing ever too late beyond happiness.

Don't give up on your today

Because of the failures of yesterday.

Don't give up on your tomorrow

Because of the challenges of today.

Don't give up on your today

Because of the trials of yesterday.

Don't give up on your tomorrow

Because of the difficulties of today.

Live your life for today,

Not for yesterday.

Live your life for now,

Not for tomorrow.

If today is good,

Tomorrow will be better.

If today is better,

Tomorrow will be great.

Don't give up on your today,

Don't give up on your tomorrow,

While you are still in search of your future.

Remember right now.

Remember today.

Today set the precedents for a better tomorrow.

Made in the USA
Columbia, SC
13 January 2024